"I wish Secret Keeper Girl had been available when our daughter was moving through her tweens."

—DR. JAMES DOBSON

"Moms today have to be vigilant in every way in order to keep the 'little' in our girls. Thankfully, Dannah provides guidance for all of us who want our girls to enjoy their childhoods and cherish the memories from this sweet time in their lives."

—DONNA VANLIERE
New York Times bestselling author of
Finding Grace and *The Christmas Shoes*

"As the dad to five daughters, I know the importance of the 'little.' This book is a welcomed friend that comes alongside parents to shine God's light on a darkened cultural path."

—CHRIS FABRY, host of *Chris Fabry Live!*
ChrisFabry.com

"This book is an answer to my prayers…Dannah gives us a realistic picture of what is pulling at the heart strings of our tween daughters…

"Do you need help in raising a self-confident, flourishing, God-loving tween girl? Then I implore you, please read this book!"

—FERN NICHOLS
founder and president,
Moms In Touch International

"Dannah Gresh has provided a practical, biblically based resource to navigate the rapids of raising a tween girl. This book is filled with helpful suggestions that are doable for a busy mom like you. To make it even better, this book is fun to read—more like eating dark chocolate than eating broccoli. Enjoy!"

—DR. JULI SLATTERY, family psychologist,
Focus on the Family;
author of *No More Headaches:
Enjoying Sex and Intimacy in Marriage*

Six Ways to Keep the "Little" in Your Girl

Dannah Gresh

HARVEST HOUSE PUBLISHERS
EUGENE, OREGON

Cover by Koechel Peterson & Associates, Inc., Minneapolis, Minnesota

Cover photo © Somos / Veer / Getty Images

Interior illustrations © iStockphoto / mxtama, bpowelldesign

Interior photos in chapter 9 by Steve Tressler

Photo on page 44 by Sarah Barlow. © 2008 Word Entertainment LLC.

SIX WAYS TO KEEP THE "LITTLE" IN YOUR GIRL
Copyright © 2010 by Dannah Gresh
Published by Harvest House Publishers
Eugene, Oregon 97402
www.harvesthousepublishers.com

Library of Congress Cataloging-in-Publication Data
  Gresh, Dannah.
  Six ways to keep the "little" in your girl / Dannah Gresh.
    p. cm.
  ISBN 978-0-7369-2979-0 (pbk.)
  ISBN 978-0-7369-3829-2 (eBook)
  1. Mothers and daughters—Religious aspects—Christianity. 2. Child rearing—Religious aspects—Christianity.
  3. Girls—Religious life. I. Title.
  BV4529.18.G75 2010
  248.8'431—dc22
                                                                    2010012457

Printed in the United States of America

13 14 15 16 17 18 / VP-NI / 15 14 13 12 11

To my girlfriends—and everyone else's girlfriends—
who've kept the "little" in their girls,
which helps me keep the "little" in mine…

especially
Kim Helsel and Lori Weibel

Contents

Part 2: Six Ways to Keep the "Little" in Your Girl

Foreword

Dear Sweet Mother—

Thank you for picking up this much needed book for the sake of your "little" girl. Let me tell you that I read it and I *loved it*. I found that Dannah is the voice that is so needed to give parents the help they need to protect their girls. My heart was so full of thankfulness to God after I read this book. It is an answer to my prayers!

I have three granddaughters (and five grandsons), and all the things in this book are the things I pray about. I am deeply burdened for all that the world throws at them, and Dannah attacks each and every one of those concerns. As I read, there were times I said to myself: *Oh, I hope she addresses such and such!* And, by George, she did! And so graciously and yet forthrightly. I think you will find the same answers to the prayers on your heart for your daughter.

Let me tell you how you might enjoy the book by sharing with you how I did. I loved praying the prayers. They were powerful! And Dannah includes so much helpful information: resources, stories, encouragement, challenges, and strategies, as well as the wonderful prayers. She is on this journey with us as she raises her two daughters, Lexi and Autumn, and you can feel that as she writes. We must support one another, and Dannah issues a joint battle cry! She cries out along with me, "Satan, you cannot have our girls!"

I believe dads should read this book as well. (Oh, I so wish I could express on paper what is bursting in my heart.)

I guess the bottom line is this: Do you need help in raising a self-confident, flourishing, God-loving tween girl? Then I implore you, please read this book! Dannah gives us a realistic picture of what is pulling at the heart strings of our tween daughters. Her extensive research, biblical truths, recommended resources, and practical, hands-on helps will bring hope, encouragement, and direction as you raise this priceless treasure—your daughter.

God bless you, dear mom.

Fern Nichols
Founder and president, Moms In Touch International
momsintouch.org

Introducing the Six Ways

✳

Becoming what I am—a mom who shows other moms how to connect to their daughters—didn't happen by chance. I started praying for it when I was 19.

Why 19? Let me back up to a really critical part of my story. And—it could be that parts of it may sound oddly familiar to you as you look back at yours.

I was 15 years old, a perfectly well-adjusted, well-loved Christian teenager. While attending a conservative Christian high school, I remained active in a very loving missionary-driven church. On weekdays, I stood solemn and tall in my wool skirt that covered my knees while I sung great hymns of the faith like "It Is Well with My Soul" and learned the commandments of God in chapel. On Sunday and Wednesday nights, I donned my corduroys and sang along to choruses like "God Is So Good" accompanied by guitar, and I learned to have a love relationship with Jesus.

I don't discount the critical importance of either of these discipling experiences. From my school, I learned to serve my God. From my church, I learned to love Him. At that tender age, I did the only thing I felt I could do with these two overwhelming certainties of service and love—I signed up to be a missionary for Child Evangelism Fellowship.

I started a summer of service at training camp, where I learned to teach Bible stories and memorized the "Roman Road." I have the oddest memory from that week at camp: Kool-Aid. Shortly before camp I felt the urge to write a letter (in case you've forgotten, it's like e-mail but slower) to my boyfriend. It was a hot summer day and I had just mixed up an ice-cold quart of raspberry-flavored Kool-Aid. I took a nice tall glass of it with me into my dad's office to type my love letter. (Yes, it was the days of typewriters!) My refreshing beverage ended up all over my dad's carpet after a run-in with the typewriter's "return." I spent the afternoon cleaning up, hiding my secret.

And when my parents came home, I lied about it.

That crazy lie followed me all the way to camp, where I called my parents and confessed. Just one little lie about Kool-Aid had put way too much space between me and my parents. We were *that* close, and I was *that* innocent!

Three months later, I chose the unthinkable. It made no sense. Although I take full responsibility, almost 30 years later I can't help but see the deceptive trap set for an innocent teenage girl who was crazy in love with Jesus and on a path to do big things for the kingdom of God. I won't share the details and reasons for the sake of everyone involved—but with a summer of service and loving the Lord behind me, I walked down another path. At the end of that wooded path, I gave away the gift God meant for me to give my husband on my wedding night.

It hit me without warning. It seemed impossible, and it would begin a terrible cycle of sin. When the reality finally sank in that I couldn't live a life of purity and stay in a relationship with this guy, I found the courage to break it off, and I began to rebuild my resolve to live according to God's loving and tender guidelines for my life.

But I was plagued by depression, self-inflicted rules of penance, and loneliness.

And I told no one.

Spilled Kool-Aid was nothing compared to the secret I'd carry for the next ten years. I suffered none of the physical consequences of sexual sin, but I knew well the emotional and spiritual darkness that ensues.

It was a long and lonely pause in my life. And that is how I came—as a 19-year-old—to begin to understand my life message. It was then that I wrote this:

-------------------------------- ❋ ❋ ❋ --------------------------------

"It's so easy to fall into bad situations if you don't build up a very straightforward defense. Believe me! I know! I was just very naive and didn't have knowledge of what was going on before it happened. I hope and pray that I'll be able to know when to guide my daughter in building up defenses so she will have a little better time of it than I for waiting. I've wasted precious years of growth with the Lord. Now, it's like starting over! That's the hard way to go. I know there is no way I can decide how things will go for my daughter, but I'm praying God will give me wisdom to be her friend and guide."

-------------------------------- ❋ ❋ ❋ --------------------------------

I wrote countless entries like that during my college years. Some were the ramblings of my heart. Others were prayers and pleadings with God for "my daughter," though she was yet to be conceived.

But there was good news to be discovered in my hurt that might encourage you. My secret sin—when I gave it to the Lord for forgiveness and healing—became the very strength of the Lord's plan to use me. It is out of this secret that I have served him, coaching hundreds of thousands of teen girls to live lives of purity. The endless hours, weeks, and months I've spent researching teenagers and the risks every parent fears were a catharsis for me. I never intended to become a national spokesperson on modesty and purity. I just did it for my little girl!

Eventually, my research led me to the knowledge that value formation—concerning purity, family structure, sobriety, and other all-too-common teen issues—does not occur during the teen years. The values are formed from the ages of 8 to 12. Many parents do not realize this and inadvertently allow the culture to speak loudly as they remain mute, planning to deal with these uncomfortable issues "later." In the meantime, their daughters are pressured to skip being "little" girls and act like they're teenagers. So Secret Keeper Girl—my ministry of connecting the hearts of mothers and tween girls—was born. (You see, I want every little girl out there to know she has the right to "keep" the deepest "secrets" of her beauty for just one man, and along the way I hope that any other kind of secret can be shared within the safety of her relationship with her mom!)

For a connecting mom's TOOLBOX

Let me suggest two comprehensive books on raising girls that could be good resources for you if that's something you're looking for.

- *Bringing Up Girls* by Dr. James Dobson

- *Five Conversations You Must Have With Your Daughter* by Vicki Courtney

Most of my Secret Keeper Girl resources are tools you can use with your daughter, and in them I try to keep things pretty light. In this book, however, I get to speak plainly about the *risks* and *risk-reducers*. I'll share with you how you can help your little girl navigate the stormy waters of boy-craziness, modesty, body image, media, internet safety, and more. You'll pick up some tools for your parenting toolbox to protect her sexual purity. And I'll share six ways a mom can help protect and guide her daughter, including how you can

- help her celebrate her body in a healthy way
- unbrand her when the world tries to buy and sell her
- unplug her from a plugged-in world
- dream with her about her prince (future husband)
- and more!

Girl, my heart is one big megaphone to God, pleading for the hearts of daughters—first my own and then countless others. And now yours! This book is my invitation to you to shout out to God along with me for our girls!

Let me introduce you to mine. I have two teenage girls who are two-and-a-half months apart in age. (My husband calls our home The House of Hormones, and he is thankful for our college-age son, Rob.)

Autumn is my older but second daughter. She is the daughter born from my heart, and we have had just a short time to learn to connect. Bob, my husband, and I found Autumn in China and adopted her when she was almost 14. Now I can't remember life before her! Our relationship has had many unique challenges, but it's sweet and filled with the overwhelming sense that God had his hand firmly upon her long before I knew her name. I love her. I will mention her throughout the book, but there won't be many stories about her since this book focuses on connecting with your tween. Sadly, we missed those years.

Lexi is my first daughter, born from my womb. She and I have a long history of connecting…literally. I called her my Velcro child when she was smaller because I feared she might never stop touching me. Oh, how I long for her touch now during these sweet but separating teen years. She's still affectionate, but on her own terms and in her own time. It's part of becoming a teen. Less touching. (Enjoy it now! I have resorted to cuddling with my 75-pound labradoodle, Stormie!)

I'm not the only mom whose experiences you'll hear in this book. I've gathered some gritty stories and advice from moms you may know, like Moms In Touch International founder Fern Nichols, cofounder of FamilyLife Barbara Rainey, bestselling tween and teen author Vicki Courtney, and more! I've also drawn from the stories of my readers through the years. From here in the United States to Australia, the Czech Republic, and South Africa, those readers have written to express their delight with the results of following the guidelines I offered in my first book for teens, *And the Bride Wore White: Seven Secrets to Sexual Purity*. The brides themselves—and often their moms—want to share with me their joy of walking in purity. And I am delighted to celebrate with them.

I've been working with tweens since 2003, and it'll be a few years before I start getting their wedding invitations. Still, I've been blown away by the moms who write to me to tell me that their daughter is "finally having devotions," or "starting to get the modesty thing," or that she's a teen now and "not boy-crazy," or is "teaching all her friends about modesty."

These moms didn't just "happen" to have great daughters. And all of us have had—and continue to have—our tough spots! But we've applied the wisdom of great Christian psychologists and parenting experts in introducing biblical values to our daughters—just like you can—and it's working! The stuff in the pages of this book *works*. So what are you waiting for?

As you go on to the next chapters, there are a few things you should know about Six Ways to Keep the "Little" in Your Girl.

1. This book is not meant to be a comprehensive overview in parenting girls...or even tween girls. My area of emphasis is primarily in the field of sexuality and purity, and the related areas of body image, modesty, and depression. What I'm going to bring to your parenting toolbox is specific skills to raise a tween girl to become a pure, modest, and satisfied-with-her-beauty teenager. In part 2 I'll introduce the six ways that make this achievable and give you specific, creative ideas to put them to work in your family.

2. The research in this book is valid no matter what your faith is, but I'll write from a specifically Christian perspective. I've been advised and encouraged to write this book for about six years, and some people have urged me to write from a more neutral worldview. "What you have to say is for *every* mom," they reason. "Don't box yourself in!"

My goal has been and always will be to raise children who make choices that are in conformity with God's written standard of truth, the Bible. That will be apparent as I write. Many of the thinkers who have shaped my parenting in the area of modesty and purity would be considered "far left" politically and perhaps secular humanist in their worldview, but I respect them, and they've brought me great insight. When it comes to protecting our girls' hearts, we can find a lot of common ground. I hope you'll see that as you read this, even if you don't share my worldview.

3. There are exceptions to many things I write in this book. For example, when I say that most tween and teen girls will struggle with their sense of beauty, I mean just that. *Most!* Not all. There will be exceptions. Throughout the book, I'll be letting you know what the norms are in terms of your daughter's readiness for talking about sex, or being introduced to the internet. I might suggest a parenting skill that will help with her sense of beauty or her obsession with television, but that doesn't mean it's going to work for your child. Every child is unique. There are also daughters who need special individual care and counseling. Please don't use this book as a fail-proof answer to your daughter's unique needs.

4. The goal of this book is not to give you methods that guarantee your daughter's purity, modesty, and sense of true beauty, but to help you to be faithful to do your part to protect her. I'm not seeking to write one of those books that gives canned rules and step-by-step instructions to create a generation of super-daughters. I don't believe there's one set of parenting methods that guarantees a specific outcome. (Kids throw great curve balls at stuff like that!) Rather, it is ultimately God's grace that will craft the values of purity and self-respect into our children.

God gave my husband and me our three children with the expectation we would teach them moral values that would help them to be physically, emotionally, and spiritually whole. With that responsibility in mind, I studied the work of respected family teachers like Dr. James Dobson, Dennis and Barbara Rainey, Tim and Beverly LaHaye, and even the work of some non-Christian thinkers like Mary Piper and Susan Linn. (As I mentioned, we're often on the same page, even with differing worldviews.) I wanted to faithfully apply sound principles in the moral development of my children, and I'm delighted with the results. I feel like a faithful parent. If this book helps you achieve the same thing, it will have done its job.

5. Faithful parents are still often required to apply grace to children who don't embrace moral values. Beth Moore, a great parent, had a teen daughter who brushed up against an eating disorder. My parents, who are *still* exceptional, had a daughter (me) who brushed up against and got bruised by sexual sin. Faithful parents often find themselves aching over their children's struggles or outright rebellion. It started in a place called the Garden of Eden, where two who walked with a perfect Father rebelled. And it hasn't stopped.

Be ready at all stages of parenting to apply grace. Just as your 2-year-old threw a fit in public and needed grace, your 16-year-old may create a scene that needs much grace. Ultimately, that's what our Father God gives to us each day, isn't it?

Becoming a Connecting Mom

Before we dig into the Six Ways to Keep the "Little" in Your Girl in part 2, we're going to build a foundation. These first few chapters are full of fun research, funky activities to do with your daughter, and the stuff that motivates a mom to press forward toward the six ways. Foundational to our girl talk in these chapters is the verse below. You might want to post it somewhere, like in your bathroom or on your fridge, so you can hide it away in your heart while we're getting tooled up for motherhood together!

> "Train up a child in the way he should go,
> and when he is old he will not depart from it."
>
> PROVERBS 22:6 NKJV

"There is so much pressure on our girls. From magazines telling them to look a certain way, to movies and TV shows telling them to act a certain way, to social internet sites telling them to 'friend' as many influences as possible. How do we allow our girls to be IN the world, while giving them the confidence not to be OF the world?"

Laurel, mom of Addy, 8
From the conversation at SecretKeeperGirl.com

CHAPTER ONE

A Mom's Greatest Compliment

✳

It was midnight.

I was at Denny's.

Having just attended my first performance of a little known musical—"Le Petit Rats"—I was invited to hang with the cast after the performance. (Translation: My then-14-year-old daughter, Lexi, acquiesced to my suggestion that I chaperone her late-night party.) She and I sat across the table from two high school girls. Both were 15. Both were vibrant, outgoing, articulate, confident thespians. One a Perky Brunette. The other a Petite Blonde.

I ordered a tall stack and sausage. The rest ordered cheesecakes and milkshakes. Then the girl gab began, and before we knew it, we were on the ultimate girls-only topic. Cramps.

"My best friend used to have like terrible cramps," piped up Perky. "But her parents were freaking because she's been, like, dating her boyfriend for nine months. They totally put her on the Pill and her cramps are gone. Isn't that cool?"

Petite Blonde got really quiet.

I didn't.

"And what precautions have her parents taken to help her avoid sexually transmitted diseases?" I asked.

"You don't even know!" exclaimed Lexi in explanation to Perky and Petite. "My mom totally writes sex books. She's not afraid to talk about anything. Aaaa-nee-thing!"

Petite looked ready to slump under the table.

Perky was unfazed. "Don't know," she said, answering my question as if I'd just asked her where my fork had gotten to.

girlhood
[gurl-hood] **n**,
the state or time
of being a girl;
from birth
to adulthood.

Our food came.

We talked about the show, our political views, nail polish—and Perky texted some guy a few times.

"It's my boyfriend," she finally said.

I had to ask—

"Are you and your boyfriend having sex?"

"Nah," said Perky, still completely comfortable with the conversation she was having with the mother of her friend.

I noticed that Petite was trying not to choke on her shake. She was slumping down into the booth trying to stay clear of the conversation.

"His parents don't want us to have sex and they've told us so. We, like, can't be alone in their house. My dad doesn't say anything when we're at his house," explained Perky. "But my mom is cool about things. When me and my boyfriend sleep over at her house, we're totally allowed to blow up the inflatable queen bed and sleep together." Her eyes grow wide. "Can you believe that?"

She was obviously incredulous that her mom was this "cool."

That's when I noticed it.

A simple silver ring.

On Petite's left ring finger.

I had a hunch I knew what it was.

"Hey, what's that ring on your finger?" I asked.

The question was like smelling salts to her fainting spirit.

"It's a purity ring," she beamed.

Silence.

"I have one too," said Lexi. "I left it at home, but I usually wear it."

"Honestly?" asked Perky, completely aghast and totally, 100 percent offended.

Silence.

"So, Lexi," smirked Perky, making a recovery from her shock, "since you don't have it on tonight, does that mean you can do it, or what?"

(Yes, in front of me, this girl said *that!*)

Lexi straightened up and looked her right in the eye: "I'm proud of it." Her head made a kind of Z-snappish wiggle!

"You seem a little surprised that your mom lets you sleep with this guy." I dared to say what I sensed.

"Yeah, well…" It was the first time Perky was at a loss for words.

"Would you let your daughter do that?" I asked.

"Nope," she said. And then she whispered, "Never."

Let me be the first to say that though I've spent the last ten years talking to teens about sex, this conversation threw me for a loop. This Perky little lady was infiltrating the mind of my "little" girl with her sex talk and profanity, and she was doing it right in front of me!

Be sure of this—*any* Christian girl is at risk these days. You cannot entirely shield your daughter from this world. I've listened to the sad story of a mom who raised an immaculately perfect home-schooled girl, only to find her sneaking out of the house to meet guys for sex at two in the morning when she was a teen. I was also the one a stunned mom turned to when she realized that her Christian daughter wasn't visiting a girlfriend's house as she'd said, but was going out to buy and smoke weed. Another mom came to me desperate to solve her daughter's eating disorder and self-loathing when it got so bad that the girl stuck a rusty nail into her arm. I know the risks for my daughters—and yours—are high.

But let me give you a picture of how it *can* be. That night I sat in Denny's at midnight as a seemingly stable freshman in high school cussed her way through a conversation with my daughter about sexual freedom.

And I watched Lexi Gresh handle it with confidence and grace.

Lexi and "Will-say-aaaan-eee-thing-mom": 1.

Perky and "Inflatable-queen-bed-mom": 0.

I felt sad for their loss.

"Mom, I Tell You Everything!"

Lexi is 16 now. Recently, she and I were recounting this astonishing conversation to someone for the umpteenth time. (Two years later, we're both still a little bit in shock from it.) Afterward, I turned to her and told her how thankful I was that she was comfortable letting me into this world of hers. She gave me the highest compliment she ever has or ever will. It's what every mom hopes for, dreams of, and spends a lot of time wearing out her knees to hear. Lexi looked at me and said, "Mom, I tell you *everything!* Why wouldn't I let you into my world?"

> "Raising a daughter to reflect your value system as a teen is—in part—a matter of introducing those values to her in an age-appropriate manner when she is a *tween*."
>
> —Dannah Gresh

It's been my goal to create that kind of relationship for her and me to share as a mother and teen daughter. Fortunately, my life work led me to learn that a mom has to start opening up her 16-year-old's heart…when she's 7! Social science offers us statistical footprints for how a little girl will turn out based on what she is exposed to and when.

For example, after two years of study by an American Psychological Association (APA) task force on the sexualization of little girls, we have clear evidence that a mother's "hunch" she shouldn't let her nine-year-old run around in a miniskirt with belted bling blaring the Pussy-cat Dolls' "Dontcha wish your girlfriend was hot like me" is more than a hunch. The APA task force's report states that music lyrics, internet content, video games, and clothing are now being marketed to younger and younger girls. The sexual content of the marketing and the products themselves—while creating no apparent immediate effect—is clearly linked to eating disorders, low self-esteem, and depression when these girls become teenagers.[1]

On the upside, my past 12 years of studying at-risk teen behavior has over and over again led me to good news. My research indicates that tweens who are exposed to a basic, age-appropriate, Bible-based value system between the ages of 8 and 12 tend to be less likely to engage in early sexual activity, substance abuse, and violence. They are also more likely to have healthy friendships, excel academically, and become positive social contributors in their communities.

It's not rocket science. It is social science paired with a whole lot of prayer and Bible study. By applying the factual information I gleaned from my research with an unequivocal confidence in God's directives for raising my girl (and an immeasurable dose of prayer), I got a teenager who "tells me everything." (Don't ask me yet how to raise a teenage girl. I'm still learning and making a lot of mistakes. But I do think I have a good view of the tween challenge you have in your hands.)

As we move along through this book, we're going to apply some of the same methods I used when Lexi was a tween—and others I've seen work well for other committed moms—to your relationship with your daughter. Our goal: to create a mother–daughter connection so tight that no cussing, queen-sized-inflatable thespian, no text-messaging boyfriend, no bong-bearing brainless friend, no miniskirt, no vampire-love-story craze, and no Black Eyed Peas lyrics will come between the two of you in the delicate teen years just ahead. While that is our obvious goal, what you might not be able to see yet is that you'll be building a strong value system *for life* into your little girl.

Getting Started

To get started, back away from the laundry and grocery lists. Head out to your favorite coffee shop for some relaxation. I'd like to hear that this book feels like two moms chatting over a chai latte and a tall caramel macchiato, and that it was fun to read. But besides that, we really do have a God-sized goal in our hearts and to accomplish it, we'll have two very distinct roles.

Consider me your "research assistant." I sit surrounded by piles and piles of research within a library of every authoritative book on teens, tweens, parenting, and at-risk behaviors I could get my hands on. In an instant, I can put my eyes upon a report called "Generation M: Media in the Lives of 8-18 Year-Olds" by the Kaiser Family Foundation. To my left is a copy of the book entitled *Branded: The Buying and Selling of Teenagers.* On my laptop computer is a copy of the American Psychological Association's Report on the sexualization of girls. I can do the heavy lifting, okay?

Your role is to be a mom focused on connecting to her little girl. This works best if you can just let loose and have a little fun when I encourage you to "back away from the book" and go try something fun with your daughter. But before we get started with the fun, mind if I let you see just how high the stakes are? Turn to chapter 2.

Back away from the BOOK:

Breakfast for dinner!

In honor of my night at Denny's with Lexi, I assign you to have breakfast for dinner one night this week. The best part? You'll let your tween daughter in on the fun. She can mix the pancakes while you fry the bacon. Here are two wickedly wonderful Gresh family variations on pancakes.

.... ❄ ....

Peppermint-bark pancakes

Great for the winter months! Chop peppermint bark into an almost powderlike con–sistency, with a few good chunks. Mix about a quarter of a cup into a standard batch of pancake batter before you cook the cakes! Top each warm cake with a dol-lop of whipped topping and a sprinkle of the remaining peppermint bark.

.... ❄ ....

Banana pancakes

These are our summer treat! Make your cakes as usual, but top them with freshly sliced bananas and whipped topping!

"I want my little girl to feel special and beautiful as God made her without being obsessed with her weight, looks, and clothes. What can I do to raise a confident little girl who eats healthy and takes care of herself without taking it to the extreme? I know my daughter is young, but I want to start laying the groundwork for a healthy, happy little girl!"

Anne, mom to Grace, 3
From the conversation at SecretKeeperGirl.com

CHAPTER TWO

A Mom's Greatest Fears

※

"Would you have some time to talk?" my soccer mom friend asked. "Sure," I answered, immediately sensing from the quiver in her voice that something was really wrong. Her daughter was 14, in eighth grade. She had babysat for me once, about a year ago. She was a sweet kid. Soft-spoken and gentle. I liked her a lot. My friend was a strong career woman who worked for her husband and had a heart to be a great mom. She was a Christian actively involved in her church.

"I don't even know how to tell you what I just found out," she said, her voice beginning to break. But she didn't take a breath or pause before she blurted out the cause for her call. "She's been dating a guy who is a senior in high school. I found prescribed birth-control pills in her pocket. They're from Planned Parenthood. I called there to inquire about her, but they said they aren't legally bound to talk to me. Is that true?"

"I'm afraid it is true," I replied.

I was angered. I remembered sitting across the debate table from two Planned Parenthood team members and begging them to at least

29

consider that there might be a certain age at which a child shouldn't have free contraception. I won't forget that conversation soon.

"I imagine you routinely provide birth control for young teens—13 and 14, right?" I asked a Bristled Blonde and a Raspy-Voiced Smoker.

"Of course—don't be naïve," answered Bristled, leaning back in her seat and confidently tapping her carefully manicured red nails against the table. (Naïveté is always the logical fallacy that the left throws at our reasoned arguments about sex. I've been told countless times that I'm very naïve, but since I've spent the past 12 years picking up the broken pieces of girls as young as 8 who've been sexually abused, and girls as young as 12 who have willfully chosen sexual activity…and women as old as 60 who aren't over it yet—I hardly think I'm naïve!)

"Have either of you ever given birth control to a 12-year-old?" I asked.

"Yes, and she was going to have sex whether we gave it to her or not," rasped Smoker. "A box of condoms saved that girl from the greater consequences of getting pregnant."

"Do you honestly believe that a 12-year-old is going to use a condom, and use it correctly?" I retorted. (The condom failure rate in teens is woefully high, largely because they don't have the confidence in the heat of the moment to go through the intimate and potentially awkward act of using one, or because they don't put them on correctly. Twenty percent of teens younger than 18 who use condoms get pregnant within one year.[1] How much higher would the percentage be if we isolated the 12- and 13-year-olds who attempt to use condoms?)

"Have you ever given contraception to an 11-year-old?" I asked.

Silence.

"It happens," said Smoker. Bristled seemed to be softening. She sat up in her seat and fidgeted awkwardly. I sensed that, with this, she wasn't on the same page with Planned Parenthood as a whole. So I looked her in the eyes.

"Can you tell me that she was emotionally ready?" I asked as tenderly as I could manage.

More silence.

"Ladies, when you give a kid a condom to put on some guy's penis, you *have* to ask yourself what prophylactic you have to give her for her heart. There's more than just body parts to consider." I said it with kindness, but in firm truth. And then I excused myself.

I knew all too well that our local Planned Parenthood was not going to talk to my friend about her daughter's birth control. It is absolute insanity that, if your child is harmed and in the ER, he or she cannot receive even a glass of water without a parent or guardian's signature—but they can, in most states, get birth control without so much as parental notification, and might even be able to get an abortion without parental consent. And here I was in the aftermath of the Great Parental Shutout with my friend.

"I can't think of anything I feared more than this," she said. "And it happened a lot sooner than I could have imagined. I wasn't ready!"

I guess that's why I'm writing this book.

So you'll be ready.

Most parents don't realize what the stakes are—or when they become a factor. (If what you just read made you want to put this book down because your daughter is "only eight," don't be too quick. *This book is for you.* Stick with me for just this chapter to prove it.) The fact is, our daughters have only a 50/50 chance of making it to age 16 without experiencing sexual sin, eating disorders, or significant depression.

I meet with parents every day who "did everything right" and can't understand how it happened that their daughter fell on the wrong side of the stats. One set of parents had given their life to missions training and hoped their daughter would be a missionary in Africa one day, since she'd dreamed about it when she was a little girl. Instead, Ivory was a 19-year-old struggling to survive a horrific eating disorder. She told me, "I dream every day I'll overcome this so I can go, but I just can't stop wanting to kill myself." She'd tried just a few weeks before I met her. (Ivory remembers clearly the first time she had the notion to purge. She was a tween.)

Though nothing is impossible with God, the foundation of building an emotionally healthy teen girl—one who stands free of the norms of an at-risk peer culture—is built between the ages of 8 and 12, when she is a tween.

What Are the Risks?

Depression is darkening the door of our girls' minds. And it may be coming about in a way that surprises you. In *Born to Buy,* Juliet Schor says, "Today's average (that is, normal) young person between the ages of nine and seventeen scores as high on anxiety scales as children who were admitted to clinics for psychiatric disorders in 1957."[2] Schor links this to the consumerism thrust upon them by money-hungry executives who want to sell makeup, clothes, cultural idols, and bras to girls as young as seven. This creates an insatiable desire not to just *have* a sexy Bratz doll, but to *be* one. The battle you and I faced when we were in our teens now weighs heavily on little girls.

The problem is not just that they're too young for the message, but that they don't have the cognitive skills to navigate the false messages of persuasion in ads void of moral values. No one tells most girls that even Hannah Montana doesn't look quite "that good" without hours of makeup and hair artistry and thousands of dollars worth of Photoshop magic. The only reality for almost every girl is that she doesn't and never will look like *that,* which creates an extreme sense of inadequacy and self-loathing at a very early age. And a lot of unhealthy habits to go along with it.

Eating disorders are swallowing our girls physically. In 2006, *Good Housekeeping* reported that 80 percent of ten-year-old girls have been on a diet, and 34 percent of tweens said they've cut back on their eating without telling Mom.[3] The *Washington Post* lamented the growing number of younger and younger patients at eating-disorder clinics around the nation. "'A decade ago, new eating disorder patients at Children's National Medical Center tended to be around age 15,' says Adelaide Robb, director of inpatient psychiatry. 'Today kids come in as young as 5 and 6.'"[4] (On the other hand, some will fall prey to the ads from fast-food and candy giants, creating the deadly challenge of childhood obesity. Either way, it's all about advertising, and that often leads to great emotional trauma.)

Not a large percentage of girls will succumb to eating disorders, but the effects are so high-risk that every mother needs to be aware of what to watch for, and when. Anorexia—excessive dieting or not eating at all—affects only about 1 percent of young women. But it's among the most difficult of all psychiatric disorders to treat. And while bulimia—bingeing and purging—commonly starts in high school or college, in girls who may be demonstrating some level of depression, anorexia often manifests itself in those *tweens* who are among the brightest students and highest achievers. This is nothing to mess with, and what your 8- to 12-year-old is exposed to can limit the risk…or increase it.

Sexual sin is stealing our girls' hearts. Approximately 46 percent of students graduate from high school sexually active;[5] 30 percent of 15- to 18-year-old girls have had or given oral sex.[6] The Medical Institute for Sexual Health has analyzed the top factors that place a teen girl most at risk of being in these stats, and a key one is "having a boyfriend for six months or longer." Without your guidance, a girl doesn't have much of a chance of not having a boyfriend for six months or longer, given the boy-craziness that consumes her peers (and maybe her) when she's a tween. Almost half of tweens have, or have had, a boyfriend, and while most of these think that means you "hold hands" or say, "I like you," about 30 percent thinks it means having oral sex or sexual intercourse.[7]

However, let's say your tween doesn't think having a boyfriend means having oral sex. Good! It could be that she approaches the idea of a boyfriend innocently enough, but even this sweet innocence could increase the risk she'll have a boyfriend for six months or longer when she's a young teen. And that's not good. Can you see how the way you approach boys when she is 8 can influence her behavior when she is 16?

Money vs. Modesty

A lot of the risk associated with depression, eating disorders, and early sexual activity comes about as a result of one simple factor: money.

Tweens are a lucrative demographic, commanding $43 billion of spending power nationwide. Girls 8 to 12 now spend about $500 million a year on beauty products alone.[8] Corporate giants are racing to stake their claim on our daughters at a very early age in an effort to create "cradle to grave" brand and product loyalty. Advertising is their weapon of choice. Our girls see ads where we expect to find them—on television, radio, and Internet sources—and where we least expect to find them—sporting events are now named after retail giants, and corporate funding is making its way into our public schools, with those who buy space in our kids' brains there deeming them "captive kids"! *It's all about money.*

I know this to be true because I've been on the front lines of the battle to subvert the relentless messages the fashion industry sends to our girls. As a result, I've been interviewed by *Women's Wear Daily,* the global bible of the fashion industry, three or four times. During one of these interactions, I was trying to send a message. After a one-year petition drive that attracted 28,000 moms and daughters who were concerned about modesty, we selected three retailers by vote. Then we armed ourselves with time and money to "shop till we dropped" in an effort to say thanks to them for providing modest and age-appropriate clothing.

I wanted the media to cover it so we'd also send a clear message to

SEXTING TWEENS

Sexting can include anything ranging from mildly sexual text messages to nude photos sent to a cell phone. It's becoming all too common for teens, and is not altogether absent from the tween demographic. One study found that girls as young as 10 have received sext messages and girls as young as 12 have sent them. What factors motivate sexting?

- 82 percent say it's to get attention
- 59 percent say it'll make them popular
- 55 percent say it'll help them get a boyfriend[9]

those who do not provide age-appropriate fashion for us to purchase. One of my team members was speaking with a reporter and asked, "What will it take for the industry to start to care about what it's doing to our daughters?" The reporter replied, "They don't care. It's all about money to them. You shouldn't take it personally. It's just a financial thing."

Don't take it personally? *Don't take it personally!* Let me pull out a line from my favorite movie of all time, *You've Got Mail.* Adorable Meg Ryan says, "Why do people always say that? 'It's not personal'? That just means it's not personal to *you.* For me, it's personal."

When the fashion, toy, and entertainment industries start to take a swipe at my girls, I'm going to take it personally. And I bet it's personal to you too!

I took the comment from that reporter very personally, and I don't mind telling you so! I have continued helping moms speak to the fashion industry under the name of The Modesty Project. Our goal today is to be a network of moms who positively raise awareness concerning modesty, encourage one another, and seek creative and kind ways to send a powerful and positive message to retailers that we want to purchase age-appropriate and modest clothing for our daughters of all ages. If you want to join us, visit secretkeepergirl.com and see what we're up to. (And I promise to stay kind and positive, but to never back down!)

THE MODESTY PROJECT

"Raising children with your values at home is necessary, but not sufficient. The outside world influences them, and so we need to influence it."[10]

Joe Kelly,
Dads & Daughters
national organization

I agree with Joe Kelly, and that's why I started The Modesty Project. Our goal is to send a message to the fashion industry that we want them to provide age-appropriate and modest clothing for our daughters. Please consider visiting secretkeepergirl.com to sign our petition and join more than 28,000 other moms and daughters.

It's Time to Take Our Little Girls Back!

On the first day I was to begin the actual process of writing this book, I started with a good time of prayer. I was seeking God's direction and favor for each word I would write. My daily reading for the day was from Deuteronomy 9:1-5. I'd like to share it with you and claim it as our joint battle cry for our daughters. What we shout through our megaphones of prayer will be something like this:

⋯⋯⋯⋯⋯⋯⋯⋯⋯⋯⋯ ❊ ❊ ❊ ⋯⋯⋯⋯⋯⋯⋯⋯⋯⋯⋯

"Hear, O Israel. You are now about to cross the Jordan to go in and dispossess nations greater and stronger than you, with large cities that have walls up to the sky. The people are strong and tall—Anakites! You know about them and have heard it said: 'Who can stand up against the Anakites?' But be assured today that the Lord your God is one who goes across ahead of you like a devouring fire. He will destroy them; he will subdue them before you. And you will drive them out and annihilate them quickly, as the Lord has promised you.

"After the Lord your God has driven them out before you, do not say to yourself, 'The Lord has brought me here to take possession of this land because of my righteousness.' No, it is on account of the wickedness of these nations that the Lord is going to drive them out before you. It is not because of your righteousness or your integrity that you are going to take possession of their land; but on account of the wickedness of these nations, the Lord your God will drive them out before you."

⋯⋯⋯⋯⋯⋯⋯⋯⋯⋯⋯ ❊ ❊ ❊ ⋯⋯⋯⋯⋯⋯⋯⋯⋯⋯⋯

The cry was for God's people to "dispossess" forces greater and stronger than they were. To *dispossess* means "to banish, to abandon ownership of." In many ways, pop culture possesses our daughters, at least as a whole if not individually. As I read this today, I felt a strong call for you and me to join together (as Israel did) to go up against modern-day "Anakites"—money-hungry, possessive giants that seek to possess our daughters. I don't have what it takes to stand against the fashion industry alone, but oh, I have a consuming God, and he is angered and saddened by what he sees happening to the bodies, minds, and hearts of our little girls. It will never be that we are righteous enough to win this battle, but *God* will win it nonetheless, with our cooperation. He created little girls to be just that. Little. And if they are to remain such, we must dispossess the media and advertising giants that seek to pressure our little girls to grow up too fast.

❋

In this book, I hope to encourage you in the act of re-staking your claim in your daughter so she can grow up to be a strong, whole, pure, and healthy teen girl, in contrast to the teen girls who are branded by the advertising world and destined to early sexualization, eating disorders, and depression. Our first goal: to help you become a "connecting mom." You might already be one. Take the little test in the next chapter to find out!

"It makes me crazy that society is pressuring our girls to grow up way too fast. It frustrates me that even among Christian moms there is apathy toward the influences they allow into their children's lives. And, of course, every mom-of-girls' nightmare: BOYS!"

Alison, mom of Audrey 10,
Anna, 6, Adeline, 4
From the conversation at SecretKeeperGirl.com

CHAPTER THREE

What's Your Connection IQ?

What do you get when you jam one overgrown chocolate labradoodle, a college guy built like a football player, two giggling 16-year-olds, and two middle-aged parents into a two-person tent during an unexpected thunderstorm? Gresh family bonding! The little thunderstorm that came our way just weeks ago as we were camping was the best thing that could have happened to us. We laughed (and sweated) until the rain stopped. Though we couldn't have created the 30 minutes of bonding that God did with that storm, we did create the opportunity for God to do it.

Why?

Do you really think I like going out in the woods without my makeup and blow dryer? Do you think I like a full day of cooking at home so we can cook over a campfire? Do you think I like the sight of my two teenage girls rolling their eyes when we tell them we're spending the whole weekend together as a family? Nope. I don't like any of that stuff, but we try to go camping for one weekend each summer because Bob and I know that creating family time—especially recurring traditions—doesn't cost, it *pays*. We get megadoses of "parent–child connectedness," and that's one of the most powerful ingredients every girl needs in order to stay little.

I first came across the words *parent–child connectedness* in the late '90s when I was researching sexual purity for teen girls. It turns out that across the board—more than any other factor—parent–child connectedness was the strongest risk reducer for teen sexual activity. That had my ear. I wanted to know more.

Parent–child connectedness can be defined as "being closely bonded by common traditions and frequently occurring activities." I think a good short definition would be "intentional togetherness." It's eating dinner five or more times a week as a family, as opposed to eating on the run or in front of the television every night. It's heading out to the forest to chop down a tree once a year because it's your family's Christmas tradition. (My girls roll their eyes then too.) It's changing your plans for cleaning the house and instead running to WalMart to buy the ingredients for a science project your fifth-grader has brought home and can't wait to make. (Hey, don't roll your eyes! I actually *miss* those days.) It's heading out to the local laser-tag arena to challenge your tweens to a sweaty game of parents vs. kids when a bathtub with bubbles sounds like a lot more fun. It's playing with, cooking with, camping with, and studying with your child. Quality time? A myth! Our kids need *quantity* that comes with great quality here and there.

Through the years, the parent–child connectedness efforts of Bob and Dannah Gresh have changed a lot (with a few exceptions, such as eating dinner together and going to church together). When the kids were in preschool and early elementary school, we connected with visits to Meramec Springs or Lions Club parks, a swimming pool in the backyard of our Rolla, Missouri, home, and tenderly tucking them into bed each night. With a house full of two teen girls and a college-age son, we now connect with Sunday morning breakfast at the Waffle Shop, watching *American Idol* together, and surviving Bob's "raft of death" as he tries to throw us from it while driving his speed boat around Raystown

Lake. (And we always end a day at the lake with a stop at The Meadows for frozen custard.) Connecting is intentional togetherness—and a lot of it—that shows up in your family's own unique activities.

The Six Ways to Keep the "Little" in Your Girl are really six ways of intentionally connecting to your daughter in a way that effectively forms values in a tween girl. I'll explain more about the importance of connecting and how to do it in the next few chapters, but first let's see how you are doing! Take a few minutes to answer these Connection IQ questions.

Connection IQ quiz

	Often	Some-times	Hardly ever
I can name my daughter's three best friends	3	2	1
I comment on my daughter's weight	1	2	3
I don't know her friends' moms	1	2	3
I talk about her inner strengths (such as kindness, mercy, gentleness) as opposed to her external strengths (such as her hair, skin, teeth)	3	2	1
When I converse with her, she does most of the talking	3	2	1
I tell her stories about my childhood	3	2	1
I complain about my weight in front of her	1	2	3
I know what her favorite food is	3	2	1
She watches most of her television shows without supervision	1	2	3
I make dinner for my family	3	2	1
I am physically active with her	3	2	1
I have talked to her, or I'm planning to talk to her soon about her period	3	2	1
She has a boyfriend	1	2	3
We watch television together	3	2	1
When she has sleepovers, I go to bed	1	2	3

	Often	Some-times	Hardly ever
I complain about my period in front of her	1	2	3
I'm not able to help with carpool for extra-curricular activities	1	2	3
My daughter's playtime is made up of interactive, role-playing games (such as dolls, dress-up, board games, and so on)	3	2	1
I talk to her about money management when we shop for clothing and other needs	3	2	1
I know who her favorite teacher is	3	2	1
I spend at least half an hour a week with her doing something we both enjoy	3	2	1
I know who her real-life mentor/role model is, and I help them spend time together	3	2	1
My child has chores to do	3	2	1
We talk about boys	3	2	1
Money is no object in regard to what she wants	1	2	3
I know her favorite singer	3	2	1
I know her favorite television show	3	2	1
When she has sleepovers, I play with the girls	3	2	1
I am actively involved in carpool for extra-curricular activities	3	2	1
My daughter plays mostly electronic games (such as PlayStation, internet games, and so on)	1	2	3
I talk to her friends' moms about parenting our daughters	3	2	1

Total points: _____

Now that you've taken the Connection IQ quiz, let's find out how you did.

Validation: *Scored over 72*

If you scored over 72 on this Connection IQ quiz, it's because you're already intuitively connecting with your daughter in the areas most critical to value formation for girls aged 8 to 12. Let this book validate what you're already up to—focus on strengthening your knowledge concerning why you are making these choices, so you can communicate effectively to other moms and get them in on the six ways. You'll love the stats, the special mother–daughter assignments, and the stories to encourage you to stay the course.

❋

Clarification: *Scored between 58 and 72*

This book is going to be a great tool for you! You're doing really well at forming your daughter's value system in some areas, but you need a little clarification because you're missing key conversations in other areas. As you learn the six ways to form her value system, try to identify the ones where you scored lower by coming back to this quiz and reviewing it. This way, you'll know where to give special attention.

❋

Resuscitation: *Scored under 57*

If you find yourself falling short in most of the Connection IQ quiz categories, don't feel bad. There are a lot of reasons why you might score this way, including stresses in your own life, a recent family loss or divorce, or not having a good role model in your own mother. You're not a bad mom or you wouldn't have this book in your hand. In order to successfully form your daughter's value system, you just need to be more intentional in how you parent. I'm here to help with that, and this book is going to be the tool that breathes life back into a needy mother–daughter relationship.

No matter how you scored on the Connection IQ Quiz, welcome to the world of being a connecting mom. It's official. From this day forward, you are one.

BACK AWAY FROM THE BOOK:

Crazy connecting ideas from BarlowGirl

For my 8 Great Dates kit on "The Gift of True Friendships," BarlowGirl teamed up with me, and we created a full CD of fun for mother–daughter interaction on the dates. My favorite part of it is the random top-ten list of fun things to do that the three sisters created on the spot. Having trouble thinking of creative, crazy connecting activities? I've got ya covered! Why not select just one of these suggestions and do it today? Here are Rebecca, Alyssa, and Lauren Barlow's ideas:

1. Bake!

2. Go bowling!

3. Go hiking! (No makeup, Mom!)

4. Buy clothes!

5. Drive-in theater with a truckload of girls and popcorn!

6. Ice cream!

7. Old-fashioned movies, like the kind with Gary Cooper!

8. Girls' "dateless" nite out!

9. Do a corn maze!

10. Get your nails done at the spa!

"What freaks me out about raising my girls is peer pressure. I fear they will be more influenced by their peers and the world than by the values my husband and I have so far instilled in them. I remember being a tween/teen—it's a scary time."

Stacy
From the conversation at SecretKeeperGirl.com

CHAPTER FOUR

Why Connecting Matters

It had been a slow-paced week at the Gresh house. Rob, then ten, had been home sick for the past few days. My boy is made of steel. When he broke a bone, he was calm and didn't cry…even when the doctor said that the severity of the break made *him* want to cry. So on the few occasions when my son felt really bad, I stayed home and babied him. This time, after a good day of such treatment, Rob's fever had broken and he felt up to reading.

"I'd love to read too," I said. "Go get your book and we'll read together."

"Mm-kay," said Rob as he padded up the stairs to get his book two stories above where I was in the basement. I opened mine and began to read. Before I knew it, I was engrossed in the characters and 30 minutes had gone by. When I finally took note of the time, I dashed up the stairs, worried that something might have happened to my patient. No worries, though. He was curled up in his bed, reading away.

"Rob," I said. "I thought we were going to read *together*."

"Well," he began, slowly and in a mischievous tone. "Have you been reading your book downstairs?"

I nodded.

"And I've been reading mine here," he said calmly. "So we *have* been reading...*together!*"

The very same week, I was making a last-ditch effort to plant some tulips and daffodils before the winter came. Bob, my husband, was outside mowing the grass, and I took the opportunity to recruit my then-eight-year-old Lexi for some mother–daughter bonding time while I planted. I gave her the task of digging holes and filling them with bulbs, and I worked just a few feet ahead of her pulling weeds and preparing the soil.

Lexi is my verbal child. In the ten minutes she helped me, she found a topic a minute to discuss. I distinctly remember one of them: "Does the grass feel it when Dad cuts it? I mean, it's a living thing, right? So how would you like it if I came along with a whacker like that and just ripped off your head? *I* wouldn't like it one bit! Of course, it might not feel it. I read that salamanders don't feel it when they lose an arm or leg. It just grows back. Do you think it's like that for grass, Mom? Mom? MOM!"

> ## For a
> ## connecting
> ## mom's
> ## TOOLBOX
>
> My favorite book on understanding the uniqueness of my children is *Different Children, Different Needs: Understanding the Unique Personality of Your Child* by Charles F. Boyd. It is one of the most referenced books in my personal library.

It took me all of a millisecond to respond, but that wasn't fast enough for my Lexi.

"Well—" I began, but she cut me off.

"Mom," she started in an accusing tone, "you said we were going to plant bulbs *together.*"

"Well, we are," I answered, wondering what could possibly be going on in her eight-lane highway of a brain.

"But, I'm aaaall the way over here planting bulbs," she said. "And you're aaaall the way over there doing something entirely different."

We were exactly three feet away.

My kids are different. That's why I could be almost three stories away from Rob while we both read and he considered it to be something we were doing together—but working three feet away from Lexi was not. Robby and Lexi are complete opposites, and my new Autumn is her own unique personality somewhere in the middle. A connecting mom has to know and understand each unique personality to be able to connect effectively.

Before we begin to look at the six ways to connect to your tween in part 2, let's lay a foundation for why connecting matters and what the Bible says about it.

Why Does Connecting Matter?

Your daughter's brain development relies on connecting. This process started when she was just a baby. In 2005, the findings of a new study released in *Pediatrics* found that parent–infant connection—intentional togetherness—plays a key role in shaping the right side of an infant's brain during the first year of life.

"We've been looking into the brain of an infant, knowing it will double or triple in the first year of life and found it is not just shaped by genetics but also by experience in the last trimester of pregnancy through the child's first year and a half of life," says Allan Schore, a leading neuroscientist at the University of California, Los Angeles. "A parent or other caregiver can provide this early attachment, but large day-care situations may be less ideal."[1]

Schore feels so strongly about the parent–child connectedness that should occur in the first year of life that he advocates a 56-week maternity leave, much like employees in Europe receive. This, he says, would positively impact the child's lifelong ability to handle stress and feel emotionally secure.

Furthering this important brain development research is Dr. Joe S. McIlhaney Jr. of the Medical Institute for Sexual Health. His groundbreaking research on the brain proves that a second critical phase of brain development occurs just before puberty—during your daughter's *tweens* (for boys, perhaps just a little older).

"Research has shown that there are two periods in one's life during which there is explosive proliferation of connection between brain cells—during the last few weeks before birth and just before puberty," writes McIlhaney in his book on brain development and sexuality, entitled *Hooked*.[2]

McIlhaney says that the part of the brain that's yet to be developed is the prefrontal cortex of the brain's frontal lobes. It's located at the front of the head, behind the forehead. This area is responsible—among other things—for appropriating and controlling moral behavior or values!

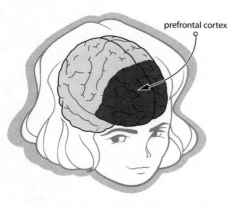

prefrontal cortex

He encourages me as a mom when he writes that "brains can be positively molded by structure, guidance, and discipline provided by caring parents and other adults."[3]

These researchers are not talking just about the emotional and moral development of the child, but the actual *physical* brain growth. What they are really saying is that we ought to be connected—by physical proximity as well as emotional interaction—so our children's brains can grow as God intended. It is more than just Mom and Dad being present to help navigate and influence decisions. There is an actual physical component involved. Your investment of time is helping your child produce the brain space to store moral values. And that gives you the ground to plant the values.

Your daughter (or son) is less likely to experience at-risk behaviors if she (or he) experiences parent–child connectedness. As I have continued my late-1990s research right up to the present, I have been bombarded by those words: *parent–child connectedness.* Connectedness reduces the risk of dropping out of school, crime, substance abuse, and sexual activity. It increases academic performance, social contribution, and the presence of healthy emotions and relationships.

Your daughter is more likely to experience positive, pro-social behavior if she experiences parent–child connectedness. This might include academic, social, or spiritual success. It can also manifest itself as a sense of caring and concern in her family and friendships. In general, she'll be more socially responsible if she experiences...well, a little bit of family laser tag and a whole lot of dinners together!

What the Bible Says About Connectedness

A lot of people rightly point to a passage in Deuteronomy to affirm the concept of parent–child connectedness. Deuteronomy 11:18-19 reads,

❋ ❋ ❋

"Fix these words of mine in your hearts and minds, tie them as symbols on your hands and bind them on your foreheads. Teach them to your children, talking about them when you sit at home and when you walk along the road, when you lie down and when you get up."

❋ ❋ ❋

This passage encourages you and me as moms to know God's value system as written in his Word and to then spend connecting time—sitting at home and walking in the way—impressing them onto our children's hearts. It's probably the most direct biblical encouragement to connect as a means of teaching values.

But I'd like to direct you to a different passage as our core verse for this book. It'd be a good one to memorize and take to heart, especially considering the specific meaning I'm going to share with you. Proverbs 22:6 reads:

··· ❀ ❀ ❀ ·································

"Train up a child in the way he should go, and
when he is old he will not depart from it."

··· ❀ ❀ ❀ ·································

The Hebrew word for "way" puts connectedness in a whole new light. You'll never parent the same again once you see this. At first glance, it's easy to see that God is affirming "the way" that is right for us to follow in general. And that is correct, because the word "train" is the Hebrew word *hanak* and would be best translated "dedicate." This indicates that our children are to be dedicated to God and his ways. But there is a deeper treasure hidden in this verse for us.

The Hebrew word for "way" used in this verse was *derek*. Literally, it means "*my* way" or "bent." It was a Hebrew marksman's term. Hunters or soldiers of that day and age did not receive a standard-issue bow and arrow with wires and buttons to adjust the bow to the man. Rather, each marksman went out and found his own piece of wood and crafted it carefully into a bow. Since each bow was made of different kinds of wood with varying strength and levels of moisture, it was likely that it took hours—days—to actually learn the unique "bent," or tendency, of the wood so a marksman could be accurate with it. The word *derek* refers to the process of learning the wood.

What I think God is saying to you and to me is this: "I've got a specific way I'd like you to dedicate your child to follow, but to be successful you've got to know the unique strengths and qualities of your child. And by the way, that'll take some *time*. So plan on investing it. Remember what I said about 'sitting in the house' and 'walking in the road.' It's going to take a lot of that."

What a task we have as parents.

Not only do we need to know and absorb God's moral value system, but we've got to be students of our children—learning their unique "bent" so we can impart God's values in creative ways that will impact each child according to his or her unique differences.

Speaking of being students of your children, put on your thinking cap for a crash course in the moral development of a child in the next chapter. I think we need to check this out to really understand "why" talking to your little girl about big subjects like boys and periods is a *must*.

Back away from the BOOK:

Top-ten family favorites

At dinner one night this week, write a list of your family's ten favorite activities to do. Make them official—traditions more or less—by writing them down. Could be playing laser tag or making Grandma's famous cinnamon buns together. Once you've got the list, post it on your fridge and pick one to do together right away!

"I am amazed when I shop for my three daughters by how adult-like the clothing and accessories are. My girls are totally happy in polka dots and flowers, cotton dresses and shorts, and frilly nightgowns. Even for six-year-olds the cultural norm is to have shirts with immodest or disrespectful messages on them, dresses cut like a fashion model's, and clothing that in a few more years sends the exact wrong message. It is hard to go backward and explain why 'you can't wear that now' when 'oh, isn't that cute?' was the message a few years before. It is harder to find modest and respectful clothing."

Ella, mom of Masie, 11, Mary Stuart, 10
From the conversation at SecretKeeperGirl.com

CHAPTER FIVE

How Connecting
Forms Values

❋

It was Rob's first day at kindergarten. The assignment was simple.
"You have six dogs that have already been cut out for you. But it is really only two dogs as they grow from being small to being large. First match the dogs, so you have two sets of three. Then, organize each set from smallest to largest. I'll come see your work. Just wait patiently," said Carrie Vincent, Rob's kindergarten teacher and founder of Cornerstone Private Kindergarten.

A few minutes went by and Carrie came to my dear "little guy," as I still affectionately call him (though he's now over six feet and 200 pounds of muscle).

"Robby," she said. "I see you have one set of black dogs in perfect order. You showed me you can do it very well. Could you please put the second set of dogs in order for me."

"Why?" Rob asked as she began to move on to the student next to him.

"Well, so I can see that you can do it," answered Carrie.

"But you *can* see," Rob said in his stuffy-nosed five-year-old voice. "I did one perfect. *Why* do you need to see the other dogs to see that?"

"I see your point, Robby," said Carrie. "One set of dogs will be enough for today."

What a year it was! That story remains a family heirloom of Rob Gresh's induction into the phase of reasoning and moral development. Thank the Lord for a wise and tender teacher who knew that the question "why" is always a valid question.

Why?

It's a spiritual question.

The art of asking why was perhaps perfected by seventeenth-century French philosopher Blaise Pascal. Let's get philosophical for just a moment. (It'll help to balance out all those days when we've had one too many peanut-butter-and-jelly sandwiches.) Listen to this mind-blowing "why":

.... ✳ ✳ ✳ ....

*"When I consider the short duration of my life...
I am frightened, and am astonished at being here
rather than there; for there is no reason why here
rather than there, why now rather than then, who
has put me here? By whose order and direction has this place and time been allotted?"*[1]

.... ✳ ✳ ✳ ....

Pascal was asking, Why? Why am I here? For what purpose do I exist? Who's in charge? The question "why" was at the core of his spiritual quest, and so it is with the millions of "why" questions uttered by your daughter.

"Why do I need to put the dogs in order?"

"Why does Daddy go to work every day?"

"Why do cats have fur?"

"Why do I need to go to school?"

"Why does my friend Angie have two mommies?"

"Why can't I eat this popsicle *right now?*"

Spiritual questions.

Each and every one.

Let me show you what I mean.

There are three stages of moral development. They help us better understand why connecting to your daughter (or son) during this end-less-season-of-why's is so critical to her value formation.

The Copycat Phase

Between the ages of 2 and 5, your child is developing a set of moral values by copying you. Your daughter will want to model everything you and her father do. In her little brain she is saying, *Mommy does it. I want to be like Mom because that feels good. I will do it too.* She is act-ing out a *consequential* moral behavior. It makes her feel good to be like you. She likes to feel good. So, she "vacuums the floor ever so happily" or "bakes a pie for her pretend family" or "soothes her baby doll" or "talks kindly on the phone to an imaginary friend."

During this season, your daughter needs toys and opportunities that allow her to copy the behavior you model. Baby dolls. A kitchen set. Car keys. Telephones. Everything that lets her pretend she is you is a good toy to help with moral development. This is an important part of creat-ing a value system in her, but it does not cement your values into her. It simply introduces them.

The Counseling Phase

Between the ages of 6 and 11, your child is developing a set of moral values by asking you *why* you believe what you believe and do what you do. It is an *interactive* phase of moral development, characterized by your child's asking a lot of questions as she considers more variables. In her little brain she is asking, "*Why* does Mommy do that? I think I want to be like Mom, but does it *really* feel good? Maybe I will do it too, if she can tell me why." She is beginning to monitor her own conduct based on what she thinks. If it makes sense to her, she'll do it. So, she asks a lot of questions—mostly "why?" You get to be her counselor as she figures out everything she believes about life!

During this season of her life, your daughter needs play and interaction that let her explore self-regulation and practice monitoring her own conduct. Age-appropriate role-playing dolls. Playing make-believe with friends. A tree house. Anything that lets her enact scenarios that require analytical thought helps her with moral development. She is truly deciding what she believes. For that reason, I believe it's the most critical stage in creating a value system. She is choosing her values.

The Coaching Phase

From the age of 12 through her adult years, your child is living out a set of moral values, and you're pretty much an observer. It's not like you're in the stands and don't get to tell her how to play the game of life, but you're more like a coach. You're not calling all the shots. It is a phase of reasoning during which she allows her values to begin to have a relationship with her behavior. In her maturing brain she is asking, *How do I want to do this? Is there something I believe that will help me decide? Maybe I will do it, if it fits into what I believe.* She will falter a lot. Remember how we looked at brain development in the last chapter? All those new connections made just before the age of 12 are now beginning to grow and be strengthened. This will continue until she is in her early twenties, when her pre-frontal cortex will be fully developed and she's finally capable of complete moral self-regulation.

During this season, your daughter needs healthy relationships and responsibilities that help her practice self-regulation and monitor her own conduct in a safe environment. (Good teammates, if you will!) Friends who have families with similar values. Chores that have consequences—both positive and negative. A budget to help her learn how to shop and how to manage her money. Anything that lets her use reasoning skills helps her with moral development. She is already living out what she believes. You are here to help her in evaluating and adjusting her already formed value system. She is living it out!

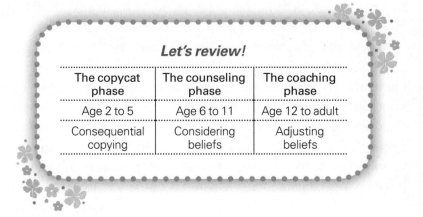

Let's review!

The copycat phase	The counseling phase	The coaching phase
Age 2 to 5	Age 6 to 11	Age 12 to adult
Consequential copying	Considering beliefs	Adjusting beliefs

How Does Connecting Form Values?

During the Copycat Phase, you're close enough for her to copy. During the Counseling Phase, you're close enough to be the end-all source of all knowledge for every "why?" During the Coaching Phase, you're close enough to be there for all the conversations as your teen or young adult hits a crisis in belief. (A note about the teen years: I spend less physical energy on my kids now that they are teens and young adults, but way more mental muscle. Our deep conversations are fewer and further apart, but when we have them they are so very critical. I can't miss them. I have to be accessible.)

Can you see by looking at this that the most critical phase for value formation is right here, during her tween years? This is when her values are formed, not when she is a teenager. If you wait until she's 12 to tell her about her period, you'll have missed the beauty of telling her that God created women to create life, and that's *why* we value motherhood. If you wait until she's 13 to tell her about modesty, you'll have missed the beauty of telling her *why* her body is good and beautiful and worthy of protecting. If you wait until she's 14 to tell her about sex, you'll have missed the beauty of telling her *why* God created marriage to be a one man–one woman picture of his love for us. It's not that you won't be able to try to form her values after she's 13. It's just that the world will have already issued a fairly strong answer to the "why's" in her heart if you haven't, and restructuring her value system is a lot more difficult than building it from the ground up.

It takes a lot of time to answer the question "why?" But it's so important to invest the time. Parents who refuse to take the time to answer the question often end up on one of two ends of a spectrum—either creating a legalistic environment or creating an anything-goes environment. Children who grow up in a legalistic environment—never knowing *why* a rule is a rule—tend to not internalize the values of their parents, and when you aren't looking they'll live however they want. Children who grow up in an anything-goes environment—where parents are buddies—usually lack the discipline to live out the values you introduce to them. You need to be a mom who sets rules and uses your relationship with your daughter to help her understand *why* the rules are what they are. And that happens between the ages of 8 and 12, when she's actually asking the questions.

As I indicated, introducing critical subjects after the age of 12 is like kayaking upstream! Your daughter's belief system is already formed, and introducing values in her teens—when she's no longer asking *why*—is difficult! So the question for you now—in her tweens—is not *"Should I talk to her about boys, and sex, and periods, and other stuff that scares me silly?"* The question is *"How do I talk to her about boys, and sex, and periods, and other stuff that scares me silly without robbing her of her innocence?"* I think I can help you with this.

❄

Now that we've built a great foundation, it's time to look at the Six Ways to Keep the "Little" in Your Girl. We'll navigate the critical subjects of boy-craziness, modesty, internet safety, and others without robbing your little girl of one ounce of innocence. Conversation by conversation, we'll explore six ways in which you can instill critical values into your daughter between the ages of 8 and 12...while still keeping that "little" in there.

HOW TO LISTEN SO SHE'LL TALK

How you communicate during your connecting time is so critical! Especially important is listening more than you talk. Here are a few things I have to remind myself to do when I'm connecting with my girls.

Give her undivided attention. Our girls want the same kind of attention they see you give your girlfriends. Don't take out the trash and do the dishes when she's trying to talk to you about important things. Stop! Back away from the Hefty Super Armored Trash Bags. Look your daughter in the eyes and focus!

Ask her opinion. We girls love giving advice no matter how old we are. You can see your girl's sense of confidence rise when you ask her what she thinks you should do in a given situation. *Where do you think we should go for lunch? What do you think we should buy Grandma for Christmas? How should we respond to our neighbor's difficult time?* Just ask her what she thinks!

Allow her time to express her feelings. Don't interrupt her when she gets emotional. Consider it a gift that she's showing you exactly how she feels. Let her get it all out. Just wait patiently and use that time to ask God how to respond to emotional outbursts. (After all, we girls are good at emotional outbursts.)

Always answer questions with questions. Often my girls will come to the same conclusion I would if they are given the chance to be guided through the thinking process. *Who else is going to the party? Will there be any adults there? Do you think you'll be safe? Are the friends at that party going to help you make good decisions, or will you have to be the one leading?* Punctuate most of your conversation with question marks and it'll help you be a good listener!

Six Ways to Keep
the "Little" in Your Girl

It's time to move from the philosophical into the practical. The next six chapters will introduce you to the Six Ways to Keep the "Little" in Your Girl. Each chapter will provide you with two very powerful tools I urge you to use. They are…

His Way

First, you'll find a "His Way" Bible verse. God's Word transcends time and culture in order to be applicable to parents in first-century Ephesus or twenty-first-century America. For this reason, there's no Bible verse that mentions Bratz dolls or the internet, but you will find verses that relate to those topics in surprisingly relevant ways. I'll feature one of these verses at the beginning of each chapter and then apply it within the chapter.

Her Way

Remember, Proverbs 22:6 encourages you and me to train our daughter to go "His Way" by being sensitive to "Her Way." You know your daughter better than anyone else and are the perfect "author" to pen a plan for value formation in critical areas of her life. At the end of each chapter, you'll find a "Her Way" assignment to map out your thoughts. This will include a prayer I have written based on the "His Way" scripture and others I have used.

"It freaks me out that our culture is essentially shoving sex in their faces—from the porno mag [cover of] *Cosmopolitan* at the grocery store to the mini-prostitute 'Bratz' in the toy store. I freak out over wondering how to raise a little girl who values what God values."

Cherie
From the conversation at SecretKeeperGirl.com

CHAPTER SIX

Way #1: Give Her the Right Dolls to Play With

Lexi and her good friend Glynn had been at it for hours. Dressed up in some sort of princess-meets-punk-rock-star outfits, they'd been creating a "film." Their roles were scripted in detail by their own sense of crazy humor, and driven by the props and wigs they'd found to support their animated portrayals. I couldn't keep up with them—they started in the sanctuary of Lexi's room, then moved to our family room, and ended up in the back yard. (Those driving by must have wondered what the blue-winged princess was doing with the black-caped villain behind the Gresh home.) Each and every moment of it was well-documented by the family video camera.

His Way

"Dear friends, do not imitate what is evil but what is good. Anyone who does what is good is from God. Anyone who does what is evil has not seen God."

3 JOHN 11

CORE VALUE: Self-control

You'll understand why the original video footage is tightly guarded under lock and key: The girls were 13.

At an age where many girls are tuning out creative play and plugging in to iTunes or Facebook, Lexi and her creative role-playing friend, Glynn, had the confidence to play. And they didn't care what anyone thought.

Children are forgetting how to play. Not Lexi. She read what I wrote above and first lamented, "Mom, people are going to think I was the socially awkward kid." Then she smirked and said, "I would actually still do that today!" She's a confident, *playful* 16-year-old.

I'm not the only one concerned with the lack of play. Diane Levin, PhD, a professor at Wheelock College and the coauthor of *So Sexy So Soon,* is concerned. She talks to teachers all the time who see the trend. One told her,

❋ ❋ ❋

"It's harder and harder to have free play in my class-room. Some children can't cope with lack of struc-ture. They roam around the room dabbling at this or that, but rarely get involved in any activity for long."[1]

❋ ❋ ❋

They don't know how to play.

Howard Chudacoff, a cultural historian at Brown University who recently published a history of play, says that play has changed a lot in the last few decades, and not for the better. In the 1950s, Disney introduced its first toy—the Thunder Burp—through the *Mickey Mouse Club.* From that point on, play began to be formed by what could be *sold.* In the 1980s, the Federal Communications Commission dealt a blow to healthy child play by taking away the restrictions on selling toys, clothes, and food directly to children through television. Since then, playing has been about toys and how much money giant corporations can make by creating and selling new ones.

It wasn't always like that.

"It's interesting to me that when we talk about play, the first thing that comes to mind are toys," says Chudacoff. "Whereas when I would think of play in the nineteenth century, I would think of *activity* rather than an object."[2] Chudacoff argues that child's play did and should consist of freewheeling imaginative activity. This allows for self-regulation, which is a skill necessary for becoming a healthy adult. Self-regulation is critical to the development of and maintaining of moral values, as I said in chapter 5. So how does a connecting mom get some good old-fashioned play into her daughter's life?

Schedule and Protect Creative Playtime

Time spent playing make-believe, dress-up, and building things with sticks, twigs, and blocks actually helps children develop a critical skill called *executive function*. This takes place in the prefrontal cortex, which, as I previously shared, is the part of the brain experiencing explosive growth during the tween years. Executive function performs many different things in a human being, but one of them is to self-regulate— or to appropriate moral behavior and values.

Sadly, self-regulation is a skill in which we know children don't do as well as they once did. Case in point—the "Great Standing Still Study," as I call it. What mom doesn't want her kids to stand still now and then? I guess in the 1940s they worried about it as much as you and I do today. At that time, researchers challenged kids aged three, five, and seven to "stand still without moving for as long as you possibly can." Just to compare, some researchers recreated the Great Standing Still Study in 2001. Here are the results.[3]

By 2001, children aged five were functioning with the self-control of a three-year-old. Children aged seven were functioning like five-year-olds. What you're seeing in those results is executive function—the self-regulating of behavior and values—in decline. You probably didn't need that study to know that kids today could use a little bit of self-control, but did you know they'd probably have better success in self-control if they just got some good old-fashioned creative play back into their schedule?

	Period of time in 1940s	Period of time in 2001
3-year-olds	0 minutes	0 minutes
5-year-olds	3 minutes	0 minutes
7-year-olds	indefinite	3 minutes

For example, if a child spends time playing "house" and happens to be assigned the task of being the "mom," she will have to make decisions about the limits of her role as a mom. Her prefrontal cortex will help her. As she's making sand pancakes for her "children" and gets angry when her stack of cakes falls over, her prefrontal cortex will say, *No! A mom probably would* not *throw the shovel at the kids because she's frustrated.* Instead, she'll self-regulate by acting like a mom. Amazingly, this teaches her self-control on many levels. (It might even help her stand still when you need her to!) It's all about thinking through and choosing to follow behavioral norms, which does not occur when play is more contained within pre-set limits.

So, turn off the Leapfrog. Back away from the Pixar computer games. Take a break from too many piano and dance lessons. Get a little old-fashioned playtime into your daughter's schedule! Be intentional about it, and protect it.

Give Her the Right Things to Play With

Now that we're on the same page about how important play can be, it's easier to understand that the things our daughters play with and what they do with them is also important. Let's take a look at a few of the tools of play your daughter needs to promote healthy executive function—the ability to have self-control to live out the values you'll instill into her during these important years.

1. The best thing for her to play with is nothing at all. The "need" for toys has been created by multibillion-dollar giants who really couldn't care less about the development of our girls. They care most about the holy dollar. Our kids don't need anything to play *with,* and they play best when they're unlimited by toys that define play for them. They'll find the props they need, without the toy packaging that drives you and me nuts. (Who on earth thought it was a good idea to stitch Barbie's hair into the box?) And they'll find the props they need as their *imagination* drives the playtime. (I distinctly remember using my hairbrush as a "microphone" when a tween, so I could perform live...from a "stage" made of my mattress!)

Susan Linn, author of *Consuming Kids,* says,

❄ ❄ ❄

"When kids play house, or space explorers, or engage in any kind of dramatic play, they are expressing feelings and trying out relationships and roles. They are learning important skills such as sharing, taking turns, compromising, and building consensus. Because expressive play simultaneously provides a window into children's experience, allows for self-expression, and offers an opportunity to make meaning of the world, play is central to children's psychological well-being."[4]

❄ ❄ ❄

In essence, Susan is affirming that play gives your daughter a chance to copy you when she's five, and to ask *why* as she role-plays when she's eight!

My dear friend Donna VanLiere, who you might know as the author of *The Christmas Shoes* and other great books, has the benefit of having started to parent a few years behind me. (Bob and I got pregnant with Rob just six months after we said, "I do!" I was 22 and Bob 23 when we welcomed him into the world.) Donna and Troy started parenting Grace when they were in their thirties. Kate and David soon followed, and it's been a blessing for me to watch as her three little ones enjoy the benefit of a much wiser mother.

Donna has all the money she needs to provide those kids with toys stacked to the ceiling—but she doesn't. She is the most frugal and self-controlled spender I know, even when it comes to clothing and toys for her children—an area where many moms are out of control! I have never seen three children play better, and longer, than hers. They are princesses (and the dish towels are their capes). They are lions (and the table is their cage). They are writers, acrobats, kitty cats, mothers, fathers, and children.

And I'm usually worn out from it all. This summer, I actually got away with telling Grace (eight) and Kate (five), that I needed to be "Queen" (of the pool). And as such, I had to stay on my throne (the inflatable raft) while I read my royal decrees (a copy of *Crazy Love* by Francis Chan). For almost two hours those girls pushed me around on that raft, making up the most elaborate stories and serving me, as good little princesses should! That is self-control in practice!

Here's the rub: When they were much smaller it took Donna a whole lot more time to *teach* them how to play than it would have taken to pull out another toy or pop in a DVD. Teaching creative play happens when they are little, and it takes a lot of…you guessed it…connecting time! If you have children under the age of five, rejoice and start playing! If they are older, this is a little harder, but you can still choose to turn off the screens, schedule fewer lessons, and get some creative play rolling.

Of course, I'm not advocating that you have no toys whatsoever in your home. Connecting kids have toys. They just aren't consumed with them. So let's take a look at one kind of toy that furthers the imagination and allows for creative play.

2. Dolls are great for creative play, but the kind of doll she plays with matters more than you might know. Do you remember Holly Hobby? Imagine one of our girls taking one of those old prairie dolls to a sleepover! You might as well paint a big fat "L" on her forehead. Today's dolls are much more savvy. And you might even say, sexy!

There's Barbie, who retains the title of most-physically-impossible physique after 50 years. If she were an actual woman, her breasts would be so heavy she'd be forced to walk on all fours! (I'm not kidding!) There are the Bratz dolls, with their street-smart sexy edge complete with smoky eyes, fishnet stockings, and pouty lips! Bratz was the first doll line to actually give Barbie a run for her money. As I write this, Mattel (maker of Barbie) and MGM (maker of Bratz) are embroiled in lawsuits because, together, these two dolls rank as the top-selling brands for girls ages 8 to 12. The only thing bigger than Barbie's...er, figure... is her *sales* "figure." (Oh, how I wish I could change that.)

Here's the deal—when our daughters play with cute, nonsexual dolls, they tend to let imaginative play loose. They role-play and create, giving muscle to their executive function. But when our daughters play with dolls that have a more seductive or beauty-based nature, they tend to be more confined in their imaginative play. Their play generally leans toward "seduce the boy." Dr. Diane Levin says, "The more time a girl plays this way, the more she'll focus on looks and coquettish behavior, and the less time she'll spend doing the open-ended activities kids need. *It puts her on a conveyor belt to early sexualization.*"[5] That last powerful sentence would be supported by the American Psychological Association (APA), who singled out Bratz dolls as harmful in their 2007 report on the sexualization of girls. (But I don't think most moms got the memo.)

This is a great place to pop in our "His Way" verse. God's Word says, "Do not imitate what is evil but what is good." I really think that dreaming of dressing like a Bratz doll and practicing "seduce the boy" falls into the category of "imitating evil." "His Way" encourages us to pursue the imitation of good. Healthy role-playing with age-appropriate dolls opens the doors for this.

I want to point out something here: You don't have to be a Bible-believing Christian to be concerned about this. For example, the APA and author Susan Linn (who also shares concern about Barbie and Bratz Dolls in *Consuming Kids*) do not share my conservative Bible-based values. Linn writes, "I often hear myself beginning conversations about sex in the media and children with the same phrase: 'I'm not a prude'...I feel the need for the disclaimer because, in public dialogue, complaints about the portrayal of sex in the media usually come from political conservatives—often from the religious right. I find that people who come down—as I do—on the side of sexual equality, for instance, and/or a woman's right to choose, sex education in schools, gay rights, birth control, and the right for school libraries to own *The Catcher in the Rye*, pride ourselves on being sexually enlightened."

Susan may be "enlightened," but she and I are on the same page here. Sexy dolls fast-forward the sexualization of girls and we—the far left and the religious right—vote no *together*.

Now, are our daughters destined to a life of shame and embarrassment as they tote their Holly Hobbys around or hide them in their closet when their friends come over?

No! There are a lot of dolls I like. Polly Pockets served Lexi well. And I'd like to wholeheartedly and shamelessly introduce you to Groovy Girls. These age-appropriate but funky rag dolls could give Barbie and Bratz a contest if we stood together and supported them. (Somebody, quick—start a "Moms-Who-Love-Groovy-Girls Facebook Group"!) Unlike the mature makeup-caked faces of Bratz, Groovy Girls have smiling, youthful, nonsexual faces embroidered onto their fabric skin. And get this—the Groovy Girl website promotes a mission that includes providing "a safe way for young girls to experience fun, fashion-filled doll play while promoting age-appropriate values and attitudes." I kinda like that. How about you?

Prepare to Say "No"

There's more than dolls on the shelves in the toy department. Some of the stuff out there is just not okay for our girls. Let me say it outright: Your daughter won't just survive, she'll *thrive* without the toys "everyone else" buys. Lexi wanted toys I didn't give her when she was a tween. And even today, both of my girls certainly have the "everyone else" line down to an art. But I have my response down too. The answer is really not as difficult as our emotions tell us. It's "no."

But I talk to many moms who say, "Oh, I fought that battle but lost...

all the girls have them." I have to ask two things: How hard did you fight? And if you're losing now when it "doesn't count," how are you going to win when the stakes are higher and it does? Did you know that "everyone" will have a boyfriend in sixth grade? And "everyone" will be having sex in tenth grade? Just how will you win those battles if you can't win one in the toy aisle?

There's no better time to establish yourself as the authority than now. Or to keep it up as the pleas get more difficult. I just want you to know that you can say "no." Here are a few motivating factors as you build up the guts to say that big two-letter word:

1. *Speak to these corporate giants with your wallet.* Don't buy the junk. Retailers only stock what consumers buy, and we can influence that if we stick together.

2. *It's your job to teach values, not to stock toys.* If you choose private or public school education, it's okay to let someone else teach your child how to read, write, or dissect frogs. But it's your job to teach right and wrong. Any time a toy

BaBY DOLLS For YOUR BaBY GIRL

If you have a younger daughter in your home, you might want to wait till she's older for the role-playing dolls like Polly Pockets and Groovy Girls. When a girl is a toddler or preschooler, she needs chubby-cheeked baby dolls. Remember, she's "copying" Mom, and that's how she learns values. So, give her dolls whose diapers she can change and who needs a bottle so she can nurture it just as you have nurtured her. (Although I for one would stop short of the baby doll supplied with a liquid-filled torso for an authentic experience. Yep—you can get a doll like that!) Some favorites in our extended family have included...

- Corolle Classic Baby Doll
- Fisher-Price Brilliant Basics Baby's First Doll
- Berenguer Doll, Newborn
- Playskool Dressy Bessy or Dapper Dan

trumps value training, you've stopped doing your job. Let the lessons begin.

3. *Use it to show her she's not alone.* She's going to feel alone about a lot of things. It's just the life of being a tween. My answer to "everyone has it" is always the same. I ask my girls, "Does Abbey have this?" (to Lexi); "Does Amanda have this?" (to Autumn). Nine times out of ten, I can trust Abbey's mom and Amanda's mom to be on my side, and it's a great reminder to my girls that they're not the only ones whose mom hasn't caved.

Keep Her Playing As Long As You Can!

You may have a daughter who is older and might be wondering if all this play matters for her. It does, but engaging her will be more challenging. The culture will tell you that it's time for her to stop playing, and that she needs a boyfriend and a cell phone. But I really think you can continue the process of creative play and protect her innocence. At the same time, you continue to build up that self-control center in her brain. The challenge is encouraging creative play without making her feel like you're treating her like a baby. There are ways!

When Lexi was an older tween, I took a puppetry class with her. We learned how to use puppets to put on skits and plays for younger children. In this way, she was "playing" but also leading. It turned into a great hobby for her as an older tween. We even sewed a few of our own puppets and bought some really cool ones. It was a play habit that lasted only a year or two, but it helped her to hold on to that creative freedom.

You might try enrolling her in an acting class, where role-playing takes a more skillful effort. Or perhaps you can give her a journal and let her write stories for you. That's creative play at a new level. (Be sure to keep them to read to her kids!) Even something as simple as putting her in charge of the creative play of her younger siblings can keep the skill alive.

Be creative!

You can do this!

What thoughts came to your heart as you were reading this chapter? I hope I didn't step on your toes, but if I did, ask God what to do with that. Take a few moments and mentally inventory your daughter's toys and schedule. What changes do you need to make to help her learn self-control through creative and age-appropriate play? What steps will you take to make those changes for your daughter?

_____

_____

_____

_____

_____

_____

_____

_____

_____

_____

_____

_____

_____

_____

❋ ❋ ❋ ❋ ❋

Prayer for self-control based on 3 John 11

*Oh, Lord! Please never let (*insert your daughter's name*) imitate evil. Instead, I pray that my daughter's play would be filled with opportunity for her to imitate good. I believe your word when it says that anyone who does what is good is from God, and my daughter is from you. Help me to equip her with toys that enable her to do good. Give me eyes to see where I must banish evil from our home so that those things don't build a wall disabling our ability to see you. From this day forward, I commit to carving out creative playtime so that she can learn self-control. I pray that you'll open her heart to my convictions about certain toys and that you'll give me courage to say "no" when I need to protect her from trends that my spirit tells me are harmful. Thank you for the chance to play with my daughter today. In Jesus' Name, amen!*

❋ ❋ ❋ ❋ ❋

"Regardless of how I try to protect my daughter from negative influences, she is still bombarded with unhealthy body and sexual images everywhere you turn, from the grocery store to neighborhood children. I want nothing more than to keep my babies innocent and little, yet the world is out to devour them. This concerns me deeply, since I have done nothing but pour positive godly thoughts into my daughter and she still comes home saying, 'I don't like the way I look, my legs are fat.'"

Tracy, mom to Allayna, 9, and Ava, 3
From the conversation at SecretKeeperGirl.com

CHAPTER 7

Way #2: Celebrate Her Body by Punctuating Her Period

There was no turning back. I was about to do something radically different. I'd never heard of it being done this way, but I was eager to give it a try.

I'd convinced five of my girlfriends that it was time to talk to our daughters about their pending periods. And I'd decided to work backward. Lexi was nine and the other girls were either nine or ten. Armed with a rather old videotape called *The Wonder of Life,* which contained footage of a live baby in utero and a few tasteful shots of a pregnant woman's growing body, I was eager to try a new approach.

"Let me read a Bible verse to you girls," I began after we were all settled in.

His Way

"You created my inmost being; you knit me together in my mother's womb. I praise you because I am fearfully and wonderfully made."

PSALM 139:13-14

CORE VALUES: True beauty, a love for motherhood

"'You created my inmost being; you knit me together in my mother's womb. I praise you because I am fearfully and wonderfully made.'" I went on to explain what a womb was and that we were going to actually look inside of one by video to see just how wonderfully created we are.

Then, I pushed play.

The girls watched in amazement, giggling when they saw the naked woman's growing belly and slightly veiled breasts.

"Your bodies were created to do this amazing thing of caring for a life that God created," I continued when the video was over. "And pretty soon God is going to begin to prepare *your* womb to do just that."

Enter the box. I'd packed it just before I left home. Maxi pads. Check. Tampons. Check. Tylenol. Check. Warming pads for achy backs. Check. Chocolate. Check.

As the girls munched on the chocolate, which I explained might come in pretty handy in a few years time, I explained the rest of the stuff. And then I told them I'd be glad to answer any questions, but they just sat there. Dumbfounded.

Had I said too much?

Was I going to regret this?

I slipped out to go get their snack, which was in the church kitchen down the hall. *That didn't go how I thought it would,* I said to myself as I collected frozen yogurt treats. Nothing could have prepared me for the scene I would return to. I opened the door and found six crazy girls in a flurry of feminine products. Hannah had opened the pads, peeled the stickers off, and was plastering one on everyone's forehead. Lexi had commandeered the tampon box and had one in each hand, twirling them by their strings. The giggles had gotten the best of them, and the questions started popping out as we laughed ourselves through the talk of life.

In the coming years, every single one of those girls came to me the day they started their period. Proud as could be, they told me that they were now officially "women"!

If you're like most women, your period has been more like an exclamation point! It's been something you suffer through or tough out.

How much do you think that might be because it was presented to you with dread—or not at all? I asked the women in my secretkeepergirl .com blog community to share their experiences about their first period. Here's what some of them said:

❋ ❋ ❋

"I freaked one morning when I woke up with bloodstains on my sheets. It was summertime and I was all alone. I called my mom at work and told her what happened. She simply gave me directions on how to 'deal with it.'"

"I was a nine-year-old starting my period. My dad was raising me. Well, I woke up one morning and of course noticed I had started. I didn't know how to react so I told Dad. Anyway, he was so cute. He went to the local 7 Eleven and brought back the biggest pad you could possibly wear…He made the best out of it and let me take off from school that day and we went to the movies."

"I think I was in sixth grade when I started my period; I didn't know what was happening. I remember it as being a very sad day because my mother got angry at me and made me feel ashamed."

❋ ❋ ❋

Forty percent of women start their periods having never heard about it from their own parents.[1] Imagine how frightening it could be to wake up with bloodstained sheets and not know what it means. It would flavor your attitude about your period for the rest of your life. So let's make sure that you punctuate your daughter's period with lots of enthusiasm rather than silence. (And certainly banish the shame!) Here's how you can talk to her in the right time and with the right attitude.

Prepare for the Conversation Years in Advance

My mom taught me something I shamelessly pass on to you: the art of celebrating life through live birth! Before you have a heart attack, the live-birth experiences I knew as a child were usually from Farmer Strouse's dairy cows. My mom would hear the long, angsty bellow of one poor contracting Bessie, followed by the echoing chorus of a handful of others. At that, she'd pull my brother and me from whatever we were doing and plop us down in lawn chairs in the front yard. I still remember the sight of that mama-to-be cow surrounded by her friends. Labor and birth for those dear old girls was a group effort. It was noisy and a little gory, but full of wonder as my mom emceed the whole thing. It always ended with a phone call to Farmer Strouse announcing that his herd had grown by one, who by then was being cleansed by six or seven rough tongues.

I picked up the family tradition, but we didn't live across from a cow pasture. So my kids had to be on standby whenever anyone I knew was expecting a litter of just about anything with a tail. There was the McCardles' prize-winning purebred who'd gone and gotten knocked up by the mutt next door. My mom's stray cat, who had to have been just a baby herself. And best of all, there were Lexi's hamsters. It took us a while to figure out that Esther and Mordecai were really *Lester* and Mordecai, but once we replaced "Mordy" with "Zipporah" we had good success with getting the babies we were looking for. "It always takes a mommy and a daddy—a boy and a girl," I explained to Lexi as we forked out the seven dollars for a pair of ovaries packaged in teddy-bear hamster fur!

See? Sex Ed 101.

I started these lessons with Rob and Lexi when they were in preschool by talking to them about flowers. Yes, I said flowers. "You see," I would tell them as we looked into a lily, "even flowers have a daddy part (the pistil) and a mommy part (the stamen)." God created everything to make life. Even flowers! Get started as soon as you can with these life lessons and they will come much more naturally.

Watch for the First Sign of Puberty

Menarche (pronounced MEH-nar-kee), or your daughter's first period, is not the onset of puberty. There's something that happens one to two years before that. It's the first sign to look for. Do you know what it is? Hint: She's got two and so do you! There ya go! You've got it. Breast buds! (That didn't hurt a bit, did it?)

Medical journals say that the average girl experiences the first sign of breast buds at 10.7 years, give or take one year. Black girls tend to be the earliest, and white girls the latest. Got a daughter like my China doll, Autumn, with skin in between? She'll most likely be somewhere in the middle. But every girl develops at her own pace, so be prepared for anything.

I encourage you to watch for breast buds only because your daughter may surprise you and reach menarche earlier than most. About 15 percent of girls experience both breast buds and pubic hair before they are eight years old, which means they're probably set to menstruate between their ninth and tenth birthday. Even if you are surprised at how soon it happens, *she* shouldn't be!

> ### For a
> ### connecting
> ### mom's
> ### TOOLBOX
>
> If you need a little help talking through all the body issues your tween is facing (or about to face), I highly recommend the deeply respected work of Nancy Rue. You'll especially enjoy the book by Nancy that I used with Lexi when she was a tween: *The Body Book: It's a God Thing.* It's still a popular favorite.

Tell Her About Her Period Between Her Eighth and Tenth Birthdays

If you aren't seeing any breast buds between the ages of seven and eight, it is probably okay to wait until sometime in year nine to begin the dialogue about menstruation. (Wow! I can't believe I actually used that word. I'm pretty sure I've never said it. Only read it in those shamelessly sponsored Kotex booklets I got in sixth grade!) Back to...ahem...menstruation..."aunt flo"..."Mother Nature's gift"..."her friend"...or, as Lexi and her middle-school friends called it, "happy week"!

The average age at which a girl has her first period is 12.7 years. This age can deviate by as much as a year and a half. The darker her skin, the earlier she'll probably start. So be prepared to talk to her no later than age nine. Here are two things you can do to make it easy to talk to her about…"happy week"!

1. Tell her by using pictures of life. Let me encourage you to put the pads and tampons down. I repeat—back away from the pads and tampons. Let's start in a less obvious place, but one that will pack a lot more power with this conversation. Why not give it a look right now? Pop over to your nearest computer and search "photos of babies in utero." Prepare to marvel!

Many moms talk about the basic function of periods, but fail to talk about *why* we have them. Having a period is God's great sign that he's preparing your daughter to be a mom one day! And this is where you and I have the wonderful opportunity to use our daughters' entrance into womanhood as a value-formation tool on the wonder of being a mom. This transition is so critical for our daughters in this day and age. The feminine quality of motherhood has been under attack, and our daughters are losing. In 2007, I was part of an original research survey conducted so I could write (along with Nancy Leigh DeMoss) the book for teen girls titled *Lies Young Women Believe,* now a bestseller. In this survey of 1200 Christian teens, the vast majority of them did not want to be mothers and felt motherhood should be a goal secondary to the dreams they had for a career. How sad! But what a great opportunity menarche is to begin to instill into your daughter the great wonder of being a mother.

Start with the pictures and accompany them with any of your specific thoughts about carrying your daughter in your womb, if you had that honor. I did with Lexi, but Autumn was carried by another, and we celebrate a woman we do not know for giving Autumn life! And we talk about her a lot with gratitude. If you're an adoptive mom, it's easy to transition the conversation to talk about the beauty of the choice your daughter's birth mom made. God will guide you as you select the pictures to share and gather your thoughts about motherhood.

I encourage you to share our "His Way" Bible verse with your daughter during this time in your conversation: "You created my inmost being;

you knit me together in my mother's womb. I praise you because I am fearfully and wonderfully made; your works are wonderful, I know that full well" (Psalm 139:13-14). This verse gives you the wonderful opportunity to begin a lifelong dialogue to form your daughter's values about *true beauty* and the value of *motherhood*.

2. Give her a gift basket with all the necessary supplies. One of the best ideas I garnered for this chapter was from one of my friends at the secret-keepergirl.com blog. Here's what she did to introduce all the "stuff" to her daughter:

❋ ❋ ❋

"I bought her a pretty basket and stuffed it full of 'girl things.' It was a fun way to approach the subject of her period, along with the emotional and physical changes that were coming! The basket had training bras, pads, ibuprofen, some new books, CHOCOLATE, and a hand-written note telling her how precious she is to me and how excited I am to watch her grow into the woman God has made her to be. Most of all, I wanted her to know that God made her body this way and it is wonderful!"

—Linda, Indianapolis

❋ ❋ ❋

GIRL THINGZ Basket Ideas

- Mini-pads
- Regular pads
- Teen-formula pain pills
- Body spray
- Chocolate
- Thermacare Menstrual Heat Wraps
- A note welcoming her to womanhood

Go, Linda! I wish I'd thought of that. And I like how you made sure to insert the scriptural truth that is so important: God made her body this way, and it is wonderful! That's the main point of all our talk about periods, pads, and tampons.

One more thing I'd add to the basket—a relatively

discreet small zippered canvas or fabric bag that's filled with an emergency supply for school, if your daughter goes to private or public school. I did this for both of my girls.

Along with the basket should come a mini-lesson on how to use it all. And since you've been doing that for a while, it'll come easy.

And if anyone should happen to twirl a tampon or stick a pad to their forehead, just take a deep breath and laugh! Trust me, it's a good sign.

How are you going to get God's values of true beauty and a love for motherhood into your little girl—in a way that will be just right for her? Take a few moments to write down some of the thoughts you had about her while you read this chapter. Take into account her unique personality, any signs of puberty that you've observed in her, and the development of her friends.

_____

_____

_____

_____

_____

_____

_____

_____

_____

_____

_____

❀ ❀ ❀ ❀ ❀

Prayer for true beauty and love for motherhood based on Psalm 139:13-14

Oh, Lord! You created (insert your daughter's name) from the inside out. You knit her together inside of me (or inside of a woman who chose to give her life so I could have her as my own). I praise you because she is so perfectly made. Help her to see that, especially in the coming teen years. Please help me to instill a love for life and motherhood in her as I teach her how her body works to create life. May she hear in this Bible verse—and in the amazing miracle of her body's ability to carry life you create—that true beauty is not a result of cool clothes and trendy stuff, but a product of your hand knitting her together. Help her to marvel at the way you created her, and help her to desire to be a mom one day. Let me teach the values of true beauty and a love for motherhood to her well, and let her heart receive it. In Jesus' Name, amen!

❀ ❀ ❀ ❀ ❀

"I am concerned with the mean girls at school who try to make my daughter feel like a 'weirdo' because she is not allowed, nor is she interested in, secular music, movies, and 'hot' young boy celebrities. I also am concerned about how often kids are tuned out from any social interaction due to cell phones, music players, etc., at a younger and younger age and don't experience true quality time!"

Jen, mom to Emma, 9
From the conversation at SecretKeeperGirl.com

CHAPTER 8

Way #3: Unplug Her from a Plugged-In World

R ob was a middle-schooler, and Lexi, a bright-green-eyed, freckle-faced, adorable tween. I was so excited to share one of my all-time favorite movies with them. They could finally absorb and handle the plotline and adventure. So here we were sitting in our little family room, and they were engrossed. I took note of my brilliance as a mom, knowing they'd be getting a message about pure and true love as they were entertained.

Just about then, an old geezer in the movie was waddling his way through an underground mine carrying his lantern above his head. Before the word flew out of the

His Way

"We demolish arguments and every pretension that sets itself up against the knowledge of God, and we take captive every thought to make it obedient to Christ."

2 CORINTHIANS 10:5

CORE VALUES: Discernment and obedience

character's mouth, I remembered it was coming. *Oh, no!* I thought. *I'd forgotten about this.*

"#*&@!" he said.

"*What* did he just say?" asked Rob, incredulous that his mom was letting it through her generally cautious filtering system.

"He said, '#*&@!'" piped Lexi clear as a bell.

"*WHAT* did *you* just say?" said Rob again, clearly not grasping that his nine-year-old sister didn't understand the concept of a rhetorical question.

"#*&@!" She blasted it out again. "Now be quiet, Robby! I'm watching the movie!"

And on we went, without Lexi even realizing that she'd just thrown out her first cuss word. Oh, it wasn't the Hiroshima bomb of the language, and she hadn't "woven a tapestry of profanity that's still hanging over Lake Michigan," but she'd let a good one fly without even knowing it.

Our children are going to be exposed to stuff. It's just a matter of how much and when. Many times, though, they will not be aware they've been exposed to something unholy, and will certainly not be able to discern how it might affect them should they continue to expose themselves to it.

When Rob was about ten, I was helping him find a website with some codes to his Play Station game. Up in the corner of the website was a billboard just twitching for us to click on it. Throbbing back and forth with electric-looking letters it read, "Click here for T&A." I really hoped it wasn't what I thought. But when he left a few minutes later, armed with the code to the next level in his adventure, I clicked on the billboard. Softcore porn. Unbelievable! Twenty-five percent of children as young as ten unintentionally encounter sexual content while browsing the web.[1]

In addition to the internet, the average tween girl watches over three-and-a-half hours of television a day.[2] At the time I write this, way too many of these girls are joining their moms to watch prime-time programs like *Desperate Housewives*. Then it's *America's Next Top Model*, where catty, half-dressed teens and twentysomethings claw their way to the top of the show. Compare the sexual emphasis and mature content of these television shows to the 1980 tween favorite, *Care Bears*.

A favorite music group among tweens in early 2010 was Pussycat Dolls. Teachers have heard little girls singing, "Dontcha wish your girlfriend was hot like me?"

Overall, a tween girl will absorb 38 hours a week of video games, computer time, music, television, radio, and print.[3] If she's at public or private school for another 35 hours a week, that doesn't leave you much time to be the primary molder of her value system. What's a mom to do? Here are a few good ideas.

Take a Lesson from Hollywood and Learn to Screen Exposure

The media world we live in will swallow our girls whole if we're not vigilant. Even those creating the images often have better screening techniques for their children than do most parents. Take rap artist Eminem, who, when his daughter Hailie was nine, did this interview with *Rolling Stone* magazine:

······································ ❊ ❊ ❊ ······································

Rolling Stone: What are your goals and principles as a dad? I'm sure there are boundaries.

Eminem: *Bein' a dad is definitely living a double life. As far back as I can remember, even before Hailie was born, I was a firm believer in freedom of speech. I never wanted to compromise that, my artistic integrity, but once I hit them gates where I live, that's when I'm Dad.*

Rolling Stone: Does she get to hear the songs she's in?

Eminem: *Most of the time I'll make clean versions of the songs and play them in the car.*[4]

······································ ❊ ❊ ❊ ······································

In 2005, Madonna created a stir that caused all too many to label her a hypocrite. She announced she did not allow her then-nine-year-old,

Lourdes, and five-year-old, Rocco, to watch TV, despite the fact she'd created some of the raunchiest and most controversial moments in television history.

"My kids don't watch TV," she said. "We have televisions but they're not hooked up to anything but movies. TV is trash. I was raised without it. We don't have magazines or newspapers in the house either."[5]

In a 2009 interview, Rosie O'Donnell, former co-host of *The View,* stated that she shields her kids from "all media." Her children attend a private school that requires parents to sign a contract agreeing not to let them watch TV or go on the computer. Since her son has now graduated from the school, she's gotten a little relaxed with the rules: "Occasionally on Friday nights, we do family movie night where I get a movie and we all watch it together," said O'Donnell. "My oldest son is in seventh grade, so he gets an hour of computer time on the weekend that's monitored. But…we're a media-free family, in most ways."[6]

> "I equate movies, in a visceral kind of way, to either sex or drugs. You're getting high. Or you're being turned on."
>
> —*Quentin Tarantino, director of* Pulp Fiction, Kill Bill, *and* Inglourious Basterds[7]

What do these A-list stars know that we refuse to acknowledge? They know that the media shapes behavior. Take for example the brief candy cameo in the movie *E.T.* A cute little extraterrestrial followed a path of Reese's Pieces, sending the candy's sales into orbit! Do we really think our kids will be influenced to eat Reese's Pieces, but *not* to have sex, curse, or take drugs?

Take a lesson from Hollywood: It's okay to screen what the media attempts to feed your children. If you haven't had the courage to do that in the past, now is the perfect day to begin. If you *have* been screening, this chapter is your big "Atta girl!" Keep it up.

Set Specific Limits

It's not just the categorically "bad" television that hurts our kids. Most of us know we don't want our eight-year-old singing along as Avril Lavigne belts out the crude euphemisms for sex right after "Hey (Hey) you (you), I don't like your girlfriend!" And we're really hoping that our child isn't one who stumbles onto porn, so we put the computer in the living room and keep one eye in that direction when they're online.

But frankly, that's not what frightens me the most. The most sensational scenarios are not what's robbing our little girls of their innocence. It's the slow drip of value-ingraining shows where girls dress up and go on dates, and our little girls are pressed to identify with older, more mature characters and life scenarios. It's what culture has deemed the "norm"— that probably shouldn't be if you want to keep the little in your girl.

One of my concerns is that there is an inarguable connection between the media diet of tweens and early sexual activity in teens. Among teens, 55 percent of those who were exposed to a lot of sexual material as tweens had sexual intercourse between the ages of 14 and 16, compared with 6 percent of those who rarely saw sexual imagery as tweens.[8] While studies often look at television shows with content deemed appropriate for teens and adults but inappropriate for tweens, you also have to consider how a steady diet of boyfriend–girlfriend television programs, mildly sexual music lyrics, and the occasional PG or PG-13 movie impacts a girl. Doesn't it make sense that anything we feed our daughters that says "be boy-crazy" would just put them in the cultural current of early sexualization?

One of the more unusual findings of my studies was that there is an actual biological component to this trend. After viewing romantic film content, both men and women being studied experienced changes in progesterone and testosterone levels. (Have *you* ever watched an over-the-top romantic movie, with perhaps mild sexual nuances to it, and then found yourself craving your husband?) These findings indicate that media content actually alters the endocrine environment and affects hormones, at least temporarily. As I write this the pediatric field is exploring this question: Can early exposure to sexual images, such as those seen in music videos and commonly viewed prime-time television, be altering the rate of maturing of a girl's body, thus creating the trend of reaching menarche earlier?

Play it safe, Mom. The stakes are too high.

So—is your daughter to be a monk? Nah! TV, music, and movies aren't all bad. Just some of it is. Here are some tips to make your daughter's viewing habits safer and healthier.

vote "no" ☑ on media multitasking!

Research proves that smart moms vote "no" to kids doing homework while simultaneously watching TV or listening to music. The brain prioritizes functions when asked to do two things at once. Since a song will be over in 3 minutes or a television show in 30, the brain prioritizes it based on urgency. So math gets less brainpower.

The upshot? The earphones can wait. TiVo the television show. Ask your kids to close the browser to the internet when they're working on projects. If they do one thing at a time, they'll also be more calm and enjoy everything they get to do in an evening!

1. Set limits in terms of screen time. With so many screens to choose from, it's best to set limits in terms of number of hours in front of a screen. (This also gives your daughter the task of choosing how she'll use her allotted time each day.) Taking into account that the average 8-to-12-year-old needs ten hours of sleep a night and should have one hour of exercise a day, most experts agree that a healthy limit for a tween is somewhere between one and two hours of total screen time each day. This includes computer time, television, gaming, and movie viewing.

2. Turn off all screens during mealtimes. Mealtimes together with parents have been proven to increase the success of children in both social and academic settings, which decreases at-risk behavior. Meals create a great time to unravel the day's events and advise your kids. Protect the intimacy of conversation at mealtimes.

3. Set a good example by being physically active and by limiting your own screen time. I struggle with this because my office is at home and I've become a Facebook addict. I have to be intentional about shutting down the computers so they're not easy for me to access after 5:00 p.m. I'm learning (for about the fiftieth time in my adult life) that the e-mails will still be there for me to respond to the next morning and that turning things off creates space for me to get active. Recently, I've been doing Jillian Michael's *30 Day Shred* exercise DVD with Lexi. (Autumn says she's getting enough exercise at basketball practice!) It's an awesome bonding time for us! You *can* turn it all off. You just need to choose it.

> "Every study that I've ever seen that's done by the networks, the [movie] studios, educational organizations, tells us over and over again that we're influenced by the media we consume."
>
> —*Michael Warren,*
> *an executive producer*
> *at Warner Brothers*[9]

When Your Daughter Is in Front of a Screen, Watch and Listen with Her

If all we do is set limits for our kids, they'll just throw them out when they aren't under our watchful eye. Remember, these are critical years when we must explain to our children *why* we believe what we believe so they'll carry our values on into their adult years. It's important that you teach your daughter to discern good from bad. This goal is best accomplished by watching and listening *with* her so you can teach her to "read" the messages and think through them!

Most kids watch and listen to lyrics and media messages alone. Make it a rule that your family watches and listens together for the express purpose of helping your daughter read and interpret the messages. That's called media literacy. Many psychologists are pressing the educational system to introduce media literacy curriculum at kindergarten, but that's one thing that absolutely has to be home-schooled. Why? Because the outcome of discernment—the process of drawing a conclusion about the positive or negative value of something, based on clues and observation—is deeply dependent on the discerner's value system. Ya gotta home-school this one, girls! Here are a few ideas to get you started.

1. Establish family TV favorites that are age-appropriate. My super-mom girlfriend Donna TiVos *Tom and Jerry* for her tween daughter, and the whole family watches. I just love watching Grace's face beam when her mom turns on that cat and mouse. (And then she goes into a blank-faced stare as she gets carried away by it!)

My friend Janet, who writes tween books and often appears at my Secret Keeper Girl Tour event, watches *Cake TV* with her daughter Lucy. It's a series that has kids who actually look like kids, with a few older teens in there. (For ideas on what kind of recent shows might be like that, you can join the conversation on my blog at secretkeepergirl.com.) In *Cake TV,* it's easier for a tween girl to discern that she is more like the younger one and isn't supposed to dress like the older ones. (*Cake* is a young teen who hosts a craft show. Your daughters will love following up the shows by doing the crafts presented.)

Also, I stocked Veggie Tales DVDs, which my kids watched well into their tweens. And I was intentional about introducing my kids to Christian

MY NEWEST VeggieTales Favorite

If you love VeggieTales, you just have to get *Sweetpea Beauty*, where the character Sweetpea teaches little girls about internal beauty. This DVD has the message every mom wants her little girl to hear. My favorite line by Sweetpea is, "God sees the beauty in things. I just choose to agree with him!"

music artists whose sound was similar to the latest craze, but whose messages were safe and pointed them toward God and godly values.

It doesn't matter exactly what you choose—just that you're intentional about directing your daughter's interest toward media that are age-appropriate.

2. Teach your daughter to pre-screen media by letting her watch and listen as you pre-screen for her. Let her see you visiting websites like www.pluggedinonline.com to preview movies, videos, music, television shows, and electronic games. This website provides complete content reviews and has many times kept me away from something I wouldn't have wanted my kids to view. Often, the things I learn there deter me from sending my kids to movies that "everyone else" has been to see.

Wait until she's a teen to let her begin to visit these review sites and be involved in the decision of whether to expose herself to something. The content on this site—and others like it—isn't appropriate for your daughter to read because it is graphic, depending on how graphic the media may be. For example, a review of Lady Gaga's *The Fame Monster* reads,

❋ ❋ ❋

> *"With 'So Happy I Could Die,' Gaga expresses her bisexuality and fondness for masturbation ('I love that lavender blonde/The way she moves/The way she walks/...I touch myself all through the night')."* [10]

❋ ❋ ❋

Sadly, online sources tell me that Lady Gaga's superenticing songs aren't going unnoticed by the tween crowd. A review like that just might be the thing to keep a connecting mom from buying into the infectious beats of one of today's most talented, but coarse and shallow, music entertainers.

3. As you watch and listen, discuss questionable content by asking a lot of questions. For example, if you watch a television show where there is a lot of dating, you might just ask questions like "I wonder why (character's name) is allowed to go on dates? Isn't she only 15 years old?" See where it goes, and let it be a chance to talk about what your family standards are about dating. (More on that later.)

Incidentally, when my girls were 13, the three of us started to watch *Hannah Montana* and *The Suite Life of Zack and Cody,* shows that were popular then (and when they were a bit younger). We loved the shows, and they're great for an older tween or a young teen, but I had them wait until they were older to watch them. Some of the programs girls shouldn't watch when they're 8 are perfectly okay when they're12.

But that can change overnight if the stars in the program turn wild, like Miley Cyrus did when she released the music video *Can't Be Tamed* in the spring of 2010. The innocent little Disney star decided she wanted to suddenly "grow up." And she did so by shedding her nice-girl image in favor of anger-fueled sexual moves in her dance routines, feigned lesbian kisses on tour, and so little wardrobe that malfunctions showed more than anyone should see.

What's the message to our daughters? That they can be Hannah Montana—sweet, funny, innocent, and age-appropriate—in one setting, and Miley Cyrus—sexual, violent, and self-pleasuring—in another? That's not a message I want my daughters to hear at the age of 8 or at the age of 17! Living a dual life is hypocritical at best and disastrous at worst... and exposing our daughters to a role model like that is to hand them over to the eating disorder clinics and the sex therapists they're going to need when they're older.

Miley might get a $25,000 bustier and millions in royalties by going bad. Statistics prove that our girls will get trashed by going Miley's way. I want a role model for my daughters who is single-minded—knows who she is and consistently acts accordingly—so my daughters can learn to be single-minded, strong-willed women of integrity.

What's a mom to do when a pop princess goes bad? Unplug your daughter from her influence. I can tell you that in my house all I had to do was follow the lead of my 16-year-olds, who quickly deemed Miley's departure from restraint as "stupid." Moms wrote to me saying that their own tween girls—once Miley fans—were throwing away their fan gear and boycotting the star without any parental intervention. But, if your daughter doesn't self-monitor, jump in there and do it for her!

4. Be sure to address true beauty as you discuss pop culture. Let's look again at one of the first true tween sensations. Even adorable little Miley wasn't beautiful enough until she was made up and had her wig on, transforming her into Hannah Montana. Then she looked like "a star." What was wrong with her without all that hair and makeup? One of the most destructive forces in all of popular tween culture is that there aren't any "real" girls out there. They're all fashion and beauty divas who dress like 16-year-olds, with shopping budgets fit for Rodeo Drive. Since an 8- to 10-year-old takes everything at face value, you'd be hard-pressed to help her understand that even those girls don't look like that until they're teased, combed, made up, and—in still photos—Photoshopped. It's an illusion of beauty whose effects will eventually catch up with her.

Ira M. Sacker, MD, director of the Help End Eating Disorders Foundation in New York, says, "Body image issues used to start at puberty, but we're seeing problems in 5- to 8-year-olds now."[11] One-third of 10-year-old girls are worried about their weight.[12] If we give them less time to feast on an impossible standard of beauty, and fewer icons of beauty who place greater emphasis on their body's appearance than on its competence, perhaps we would see a decline in depression associated with body image, and even in eating disorders.

Again, ask questions. Questions that make your daughter think— not statements—are the key to opening her heart to your values. When you're watching a show where the girls are always fashion plates you might ask, "Do you ever wonder why (character's name) has so many clothes? I've never seen her wear the same thing twice!" This discussion can open the door to a conversation about how very much the fashion and beauty we see in the media is an illusion. You may eventually be able to make a statement like, "It would be fun to have an unlimited wardrobe like (character's name) gets from her Hollywood producers for free. But then again, there are better things to do with your money than buy clothes. Can you think of any?" (See that? Keep the questions rolling!)

Get a Filter on Your Family Computers

This point of action is non-negotiable. Having an unfiltered computer isn't much different from storing a couple copies of *Playgirl* and *Penthouse* in a manila folder on your desk. Since the FCC refuses to control or regulate porn sites to protect children, you are the only defense for your kids. Porn and sexual chat rooms are *easy* to get to. For tweens, I recommend Safe Eyes (safeeyes.com), because you can block specific content fairly effectively and set personal time limits for each family user.

Your goal in establishing limits and teaching your girl to discern among media is ultimately obedience to God. While she is in your house, you have some control over how obedient she is to you. But isn't a greater goal of parenting to teach her to be obedient to God when you are *not* regulating her behaviors? *The Message* version of our "His Way" verse, 2 Corinthians 10:3-6, says,

❊ ❊ ❊

"The world is unprincipled. It's dog-eat-dog out there! The world doesn't fight fair. But we don't live or fight our battles that way—never have and never will. The tools of our trade aren't for marketing or manipulation, but they are for demolishing that entire massively corrupt culture. We use our powerful God-tools for smashing warped philosophies, tearing down barriers erected against the truth of God, fitting every loose thought and emotion and impulse into the structure of life shaped by Christ. Our tools are ready at hand for clearing the ground of every obstruction and building lives of obedience into maturity."

❊ ❊ ❊

There's no arguing that the entertainment world is "unprincipled" and seeks only to manipulate us and our children. God has given you every tool needed to smash the warped philosophies of the likes of Lady Gaga and to tear down the barriers erected by Hollywood against God's truths about purity and true beauty. He desires that we let Christ—not the culture—shape every thought and emotion!

How ya doin' with that, Mom?

I mean Y-O-U personally. Is Christ shaping your sense of beauty? Or is the culture?

Don't be too hard on yourself in this area. It's so easy to get caught up in our culture. As I've been writing this chapter, I've felt convicted to look at our family limits and address where we've been slipping. If you feel some of that kind of concern, it's okay. Take a few moments and write down some specific things on your heart, things you need to modify. Take into consideration what your daughter is currently exposed to, and which things should be addressed first. Consider how you can involve her dad in any changes you feel led to make.

_____

_____

_____

_____

_____

_____

_____

_____

❊ ❊ ❊ ❊ ❊

Prayer for discernment and obedience
based on 2 Corinthians 10:5

Oh, Lord! When I really step back and examine the culture, I realize it's unprincipled. I want to ask you to teach me how to fight the media battles my daughter faces. You have given me tools through your Word and prayer to smash warped philosophies and to tear down those things in my daughter's life that have been erected against your truth. Help me to train her to make every thought and emotion a response to Christ, because her life is shaped by him. I ask you to help me teach (insert your daughter's name) *to be discerning in her media choices and to be obedient to you in everything she exposes herself to. In Jesus' Name, amen!*

❊ ❊ ❊ ❊ ❊

VICKI courtney on FIGHTING THE MEDIA

Dannah: Vicki, your daughter Paige is now a young adult. What's something you did to help her in her tween years when celebrity images assaulted her sense of beauty?

Vicki: We memorized Psalm 139:14 and had a silly game we played. If one of us would diss ourselves, the other would say, "Repeat after me: 'I praise you because I am fearfully and wonderfully made; Your works are wonderful, I know that full well.'" (For the record, Paige seemed to enjoy being able to remind me!) Paige is now 19, and recently I repeated our old line. Her cousin was with us and burst out laughing when I quoted it in a schoolmarmish tone of voice. Paige replied by saying, "See what I had to live with…" But hey, she has a very healthy body image overall, so I have no regrets!

Dannah: Were there times when fashion got in the way of true beauty and modesty?

Vicki: Paige was a tween in what I call the Britney-Spears-inspired-bare-midriff era. Fun times! I put my foot down at the tight tees that were made to crop above the waistband. Even so, it was still a constant battle. Paige wasn't one to really push boundaries, but sometimes she would come home in borrowed fashions from friends or her shirts would truly shrink in the dryer. I continued to remind her of the "why" behind God's standard for modesty in an effort to counteract the wishy-washy message coming from the media.

Dannah: So it's okay to say "no" to some fashions?

Vicki: Yes-sir-ree!

I highly recommend Vicki's magabooks for tweens! **Between** *and* **Between Us Girls** *are both magazine-style books filled with great Bible truth for your daughter. For more information, go to vickicourtney.com.*

"How can moms think that letting their elementary-age daughters read fashion magazines geared toward teens or magazines about pop stars at such a young age is healthy? Am I the only one who thinks this stuff is trash and the LIBRARY is the place to get quality reading material?"

Ella, mom of Masie, 11,
Mary Stuart, 10
From the conversation at SecretKeeperGirl.com

CHAPTER NINE

Way #4: Unbrand Her When the World Tries to Buy and Sell Her

"Lexi, it's 80 degrees out," I exclaimed. "Why don't you put on some shorts?"

"Nope," she said. "Pants are good."

It would be another year before I discovered the cause of Lexi's obsession with pants. During a "date" with her (from *8 Great Dates for Moms and Daughters,* an interactive resource I'd recently written), Lexi opened her heart to tell me that she really disliked her legs. We prayed over it, and I begged the God of heaven to help her to see how beautiful she was and was

His Way

"Your beauty should not come from outward adornment, such as braided hair and the wearing of gold jewelry and fine clothes. Instead, it should be that of your inner self, the unfading beauty of a gentle and quiet spirit, which is of great worth in God's sight."

1 PETER 3:3-4

CORE VALUES: Inner beauty, modesty, contentment

becoming each day. He must have gotten to it right away. A few weeks later, we had another memorable conversation.

"Mom," piped my sweet ten-year-old. "How old do I hafta be before I start to shave like you?"

The look on that little freckled face told me a whole lot more than her words.

"Did you just shave?" I asked.

"Yup!" she answered, beaming with pride.

"Well," I said. "I guess you 'hafta' be ten."

Lexi started wearing shorts. A few weeks later the novelty of shaving wore off and she went natural again, but she never went back to her obsession with pants.

It all started with Marilyn Monroe in the 1950s. Her voluptuous curves and plump red lips became the new standard of beauty. Men wanted her. Women wanted to look like her, and so her name and face were used to sell anything and everything to women. At the height of her beauty-symbol status, Monroe was photographed in that famous blown-dress pose. She was 28.

Apparently there wasn't enough money to be made on adult women. Finally, a term coined by Madison Avenue in 1941—*teenager*—would become a sales demographic. Welcome Brooke Shields to the scene, who provocatively purred, "Nothing comes between me and my Calvins"—meaning Calvin Klein jeans—in 1980. She was 15.

And it still hasn't been enough. The new millennium brought us to a new low for sales and marketing when the term *tween* was coined. (It was a long time coming. A marketing giant named Eugene Gilbert called them "sub-teens" and said in 1962 that the retailer who taps into this market "can look forward to an unparalleled business potential.") Welcome Miley Cyrus to the scene, who became the culture's first image-peddling 13-year-old.

And parents have literally bought into it. In 2009, the 8-to-12-year-old demographic—with a name that has finally stuck, tweens—spent a whopping $43 billion nationwide on things like clothing, food, toys, electronics and, let's not forget, cell phones. Worldwide it was something like $170 billion. (And that doesn't include the "pester power" tweens use to help make decisions about larger purchases like vacations and family cars.)

For girls, the pressure is relentless to try on and wear clothes designed to highlight female allure, and to desire other beauty products they don't even need. As I said before, the findings of the two-year study by the APA on the sexualization of girls found that the marketing associated with these products—and the products themselves—are linked to eating disorders, low self-esteem, depression, and early sexual activity. Instead of making girls feel good about their bodies, they end up feeling fat or unattractive. Instead of taking on romantic relationships at an age when they are ready, they do it too soon and then are emotionally scarred by the time they meet the man of their dreams. Instead of continuing the value formation of self-control, they're disrupted by excessive materialism.

It's time for you and me to say, "Enough is enough! Seven will not be the new sixteen!" To unbrand our daughters, we have to address the two-headed serpent of excessive materialism and early sexualization. We do this by reclaiming the biblical values of contentment, which produces a giving heart, and modesty, which produces a virtuous life.

Practice Modesty and Humility in Front of Her Every Day

Let's take a closer look at "His Way": "Your beauty should not come from outward adornment, such as braided hair and the wearing of gold jewelry and fine clothes. Instead, it should be that of your inner self, the unfading beauty of a gentle and quiet spirit which is of great worth in God's sight." This verse doesn't tell us that we can't shop a little for cute clothes, wear awesome jewelry, or sport a super cut. It just says that the source of our beauty isn't in those things but on the inside, where it can't fade.

Your daughter isn't going to see the value of inner beauty in pop culture. Nor is she going to hear anything about modesty. She's got to see those traits in *you*. That means *you* need to dress modestly. *You* need to live in humility with a spirit of contentment that's visible through a life of giving. (When was the last time your daughter helped you do an act of kindness?)

A critical evidence of your modesty and humility will be a contentment not only with what you have, but with how you were created. Hear me on this, Mom: That means you won't walk around criticizing your own body in front of her. "I'm fat." "Do I look fat?" "I have *got* to work out!" "My skin is a mess!" These statements may be true to how you feel—and even be some areas where you need to focus some discipline and attention—but research suggests that daughters who hear their moms criticize their own bodies are less confident about their own. (That's why I asked you at the close of the last chapter how your own sense of beauty was standing up against the culture's impossible standards!)

We will struggle with our sense of beauty in a world that doesn't honor true beauty, because we can never look like the magazine-cover models. (*They* don't even look like that!) Just this morning, I was reading a copy of *New Beauty* magazine as part of my research for this book. After pages and pages of "before" and "after" cosmetic-surgery pictures, I decided I needed a tummy tuck and a breast lift! Then the irony that I was writing a chapter on embracing true beauty dawned on me. No matter how much we believe in and feast on God's truth about beauty, our existence in a fallen world will always give us something to obsess about. (I decided to just stick with Pilates.)

BODY mass mayhem

Do your daughters—and you— see healthy images in the models who sell us all this stuff? Nope! A healthy body mass index is anywhere between 18.5 and 25. Of today's top supermodels, only Heidi Klum reports a BMI even close to this range!

Heidi Klum, 18
Paris Hilton, 16
Nicole Richie, 17
Kate Moss, 15.7
Gisele Bundchen, 17.4
Lily Cole, 15.6[1]

How do you cause a modest and content spirit to grow in your daughter? You cultivate one in yourself first. So roll up your sleeves with me when we get to the "True Beauty Challenge" in a few pages.

Teach Her My "Truth or Bare Fashion Tests" When She's Eight

Many moms make the mistake of waiting until their daughter is developing breasts and curves to begin introducing the concept of modesty. Big mistake. Two things happen when you wait too long. First, you often miss the critical value-formation years when she's asking "why" with an open spirit and mind. Second, you inadvertently send a message that her body is bad. Since she already may feel self-conscious about the changes taking place, it's better to introduce modesty before that happens so the message is clear: Some clothes are bad, but your body is a masterpiece created by God!

So, how do you introduce the idea of modesty to an eight-year-old, for crying out loud? My "crazy friend" and Secret Keeper Girl fiction author and teacher Janet Mylin and I developed the first of my Truth or Bare Fashion Tests for a little fashion show we were doing about eight years ago. The tests have taken on a life of their own as I've added to them through the years. I receive letters of apology from published authors who've used them and then found out where they came from. I don't really care that they're published without credit. I just want them to be *used*. How have they gotten a life of their own? They're *fun!*

The absolute best way to experience them is live at a Secret Keeper Girl event, but you can also introduce them very effectively using one of my Secret Keeper Girl 8 Great Date resources. There's one on modesty and true beauty, and one on true friendships. Both contain creative instructions on how to share these with your daughter.

But if you just want to wing it, they're posted in full color at www.secretkeepergirl.com, and here they are in black and white.

THE TRUTH OR BARE
FASHION TESTS

The raise and praise test

Target: Am I showing too much belly?

Action: Stand straight up, pretend you are "going for it" in worship, and extend your arms in the air to God. Is this exposing a lot of belly? Bellies are very beautiful, and they need to be saved for our husband.

Remedy: Go to the guy's department and buy a simple ribbed tank T-shirt to wear under your funky short T's or with your trendy low-riders. Layers are a great solution to belly shirts. I call tank T-shirts a girl's "secret weapon." You should have lots of these because you can use them in many ways, as you'll soon see.

The mirror, mirror test

Target: How short is too short?

Action: Get in front of a full-length mirror. If you are in shorts, sit criss-cross applesauce style. If you are in a skirt, sit in a chair with your legs crossed. Now, what do you see in that mirror? If it's the stripes or flowers on your panties, your shorts or skirt is too short.

Remedy: Buy longer shorts and skirts. If you really love a skirt that's not too short, but you can't sit well in it without showing off your undies, try pairing it with leggings.

The "I see London, I see France" test

Target: Can you see my underpants?

Action: Bend over and touch your knees. Have a friend look right at your bottom. Can she see the outline of your underpants or the seams in them? How about the color in them? Can she see your actual underwear because your pants are so low that you're risking a "plumber" exposure?

Remedy: Wear white "granny panties" with white shorts, skirts, pants, and even jeans. If your pants are so tight that you can see the outline of your panties, you need to try buying one size larger. And, if you're pulling a plumber, try our "secret weapon."

The over & out test

Target: Is my shirt too low?

Action: No one really lives standing straight up. We bend and stretch and move, and sometimes our clothes do too! Lean over a little bit. If there is too much chest skin showing (where future cleavage will be), your shirt is too low.

Remedy: Today's fashions thrive on low shirts. Layering them is often the only remedy. Throw a little T-shirt under a rugby, and you have a great look!

The "spring valley" test

Target: Is my shirt too tight?

Action: Before I tell you how to take this test, I should tell you that your daughter probably doesn't need it yet. (But you do.) Place the tips of your fingers together and press into your shirt right in the "valley" between the breasts! Count to three and take your fingers away quickly. If your shirt springs back with a G-force that would kill a small rodent, it is probably too tight! Lots of Christian woman and teens don't show off too much skin, but they show off too much shape.

Remedy: Buy a bigger shirt! Don't buy shirts based on size. Buy them based on fit. I'm often bothered that I have to buy an XL or XXL T-shirt, when in reality I wear a size 8 blouse. (Janet's advice is to use a Sharpie marker to make it any size I want it to be. Something like "Size: 100 percent Bob's Totally Hot Wife" usually does the trick for me!)

Here's the really critical thing about the Truth or Bare Fashion Tests—you have to model them if you want her to embrace them. So go ahead. Find a room that's private and give it a go.

I'm serious.

Go try it out right now.

…Okay, how'd you do?

If you didn't pass, trash some of your clothes and treat yourself to some shopping soon. Here is where the rubber meets the road when you're instilling the value of modesty into your daughter. You have to model it.

Take the True Beauty Challenge Together

This tip is the most important one in this chapter. If you'll do this one thing, you can dramatically increase your daughter's chances of surviving her teen years without experiencing self-loathing, eating disorders, and depression. A little bit of encouragement...my Lexi is one of the most confident young teens I've ever met. She isn't genetically perfect—though she is beautiful—but she is overcoming the self-loathing we faced together when she was a tween. I'm confident that is, in part, due to our True Beauty Challenge. Based on 1 Peter 3:3-4 ("His Way"), the challenge is to ask yourself every single day, "Did I spend more time in front of the mirror making myself externally beautiful, or did I spend more time developing my inner beauty through quiet communion with God?" It's that easy.

You see, if you spend one hour getting your face and body groomed for the day, but fail to spend one hour in God's Word grooming your spirit, you are setting yourself up to believe the lies of the world. Make a new goal for yourself—and help your tween daughter establish the habit of spending more time in God's Word each day than she does in front of the mirror. It's easy—if you spend 15 minutes getting ready each morning, you need to spend 15 minutes with God. If you spend 30 minutes painting your face and spraying your hair, you need to spend 30 minutes with God.

I have many tools on my website to help you achieve this goal, including a great mother–daughter devotional. And all of my 8 Great Date resources have devotional components that make it easy to help your tween dig in!

Her Way

Have you been living a life of modesty in front of your daughter? I hope so. If not, it isn't too late to start today. Being sensitive to your daughter's personality, what steps do you need to take to help her embrace inner beauty as a greater value than external beauty? Consider taking the True Beauty Challenge by getting yourself and your daughter into the Word of God for more minutes a day than you spend in front of the mirror. How can you begin to do this?

_____

_____

_____

_____

_____

_____

_____

_____

_____

_____

_____

_____

_____

❀ ❀ ❀ ❀ ❀

Prayer for inner beauty, modesty, and contentment
based on 1 Peter 3:3-4

Oh my great Creator—you created my precious daughter, and therefore (insert your daughter's name) *is perfectly as you intended her to be. I plead with you to speak to her heart and give her a passion to have internal beauty in the form of a gentle and quiet spirit, because this is of great worth to you. Please help me to teach her to say "no" to the world's outward adornment—haircuts, excessive jewelry, obsession with clothing. May she be content with what she has and modest in how she expresses her beauty. Oh, do not let the enemy of her soul lie to her about how perfectly created she is. And if he does, I pray that I will have faithfully planted your truth inside of her so she can recognize his lies. Thank you for my beautiful daughter. In Jesus' Name, amen!*

❀ ❀ ❀ ❀ ❀

Suzy Weibel
on the
Greedy-Grimy
Gimmes

Dannah: It seems like way too many of our daughters get a bad case of the Greedy-Grimy Gimmes in their tween or teen years. What's something you've done to avoid that with your girls?

Suzy: I'm a Financial Peace University mom! All through their teen years my girls—Rachael and Marie—have received a "budget" rather than an allowance. The idea is that their budget is enough to cover what they need throughout the month. They are responsible for all their clothing purchases. That puts the kibosh on impulse buying.

Dannah: Any other benefits to budgeting?

Suzy: Budgeting includes saving and tithing, which come first, and once your daughter gets the thrill of those two things she'll be quick to do it. Rachael is now a young adult who is waitressing. She is living off her tips and putting 100 percent of her paycheck into savings. She "gets" it!

Dannah: Do you think you can introduce that kind of budgeting during a girl's tween years?

Suzy: Absolutely! When she is a tween, you can put an envelope above her bed with the word "tithe" on it for her to fill each week, and you can encourage her to save regularly. This encourages an attitude of giving.

You may meet Suzy at one of my live Secret Keeper Girl Tour events. If you're raising a girl who loves sports, you should have T is for Antonia, *Suzy's fiction book for tweens, in your daughter's library! For more information, go to www.secret keepergirl.com.*

"I'm concerned that my child is naive and innocent, as she should be at eight years old, but could be influenced by peers."

Jamie
From the conversation at SecretKeeperGirl.com

CHAPTER TEN

Way #5: Become the Carpool Queen and Sleepover Diva

Flash back with me to 1980, where I am sporting a Farrah Fawcett–inspired feathered haircut, "going with" the second most popular guy at Fairmount Elementary, and enjoying a measure of popularity myself even though my dad won't let me wear clogs. The *most* popular guy at school, Blake, has just moved, and we are experiencing no small amount of sixth-grade devastation.

We do the only thing we can think to do. We all write him letters. (A bit old-fashioned, I know. Could we have just kept up with him in Facebook, I'm sure we'd have done it that way!) At the end of the day, I collect the letters and take them home to mail them. My mom, after all, is practically

His Way

"He who walks with the wise grows wise, but a companion of fools suffers harm."

PROVERBS 13:20

VALUES FORMED: Wisdom, positive peer pressure

the class mascot. She's the Carpool Queen and Sleepover Diva of middle school. I know she'll be happy to get involved.

And she was.

She took one look at letter after letter, which had all been signed "High and Horny," and told me she had to call everyone's parents. And she did.

It took me about three years to figure out what "high" meant. The latter didn't really sink in until I was in college. But losing my status as a popular girl took about one hour.

> "One of the things my children left behind when they flew the coop was a billion miles on my '91 Mooremobile. OK. So it was only 127,000. But I felt every mile of it. In fact, I'm still feeling it since I'm still driving it…130,000 miles and counting."
>
> —Bestselling author Beth Moore (a.k.a. Carpool Queen!)[2]

Learn How Friends Form Values

Welcome to the years of *homophily*. That's a fancy psych term for cliques. While I don't like cliques, and we've worked hard to keep our kids from forming them, they are inevitable. And they can even do some good. Somewhere around the tween years, kids start to select people who are like them to be their friends. Conversely, whoever they pick to be their friends will affect who they become. Friendships formed in the tween and teen years have significant influence on behaviors in the areas of violence, sexuality, substance use, weight behaviors, and depression. They also affect pro-social behavior in the areas of academics, volunteer work, and health.[1] Like it or not, your daughter's friends will either support the values you are attempting to instill or overwhelm them with a different point of view.

This chapter is especially critical if your daughter attends public school.

As parents, Bob and I have been fairly open-minded about schooling. Our children have enjoyed public, Christian (Protestant), Catholic, and home school as well as private tutoring. Our philosophy has been to be obedient to God's Spirit in determining where each child needed to be at the time. We're not anti–public school, but we have been extra vigilant when our kids have been involved there. It can't be denied that the biblical values we want them to embrace are not supported in that environment.

And since public-school children come from homes with a wider variety of worldviews, your daughter can be exposed to just about anything in her friendships. Nearly every mom whose daughter is in a public-school setting—if you plan to continue that type of schooling into the middle-school years—might want to watch a graphic and all-too-often realistic movie entitled *Thirteen*. It portrays the all-too-quick transformation of a girl who is playing with Barbies on her first day of middle school but gets caught up in the wrong crowd. She ends up using drugs, stealing clothing, and giving oral sex within just a few short months. The girl's mom is conflicted about how this drastic change could have happened to her baby. I deal with parents every day who find themselves in this same place.

Do everything you can to learn about the risk of bad friendships and the hope of good friendships in your daughter's life. This information will motivate you to get involved.

Get Involved in Her Friendships

Little did I know that my mom's uncontested titles of Carpool Queen and Sleepover Diva were critical maneuvers in protecting *her* little public-school girl—me! Part of me wanted more space, but most of me loved that my mom was the mom everyone could really talk to. (She's still like that. The other day I told her how overwhelmed I was with life. She scheduled lunch with me and said, "Bring a bucket of thoughts. We'll empty it out!") In fifth and sixth grade, my friends exposed their drama to her as if she were a highly paid counselor. As a result, she was on the inside of our major decisions. It also gave her the knowledge to step in if I was making wrong decisions, such as selecting some friends in sixth grade with a much broader and potentially dangerous vocabulary and life experience than my own.

I never was as popular again.

By cutting me off from the friends who either knew more than or thought they knew more than I did, she was forcing me to find wise friends to walk with. Today, I'm pretty grateful for the tough decisions my mom made as she witnessed the inner workings of my misguided friendships. I look back at the friendships I eventually found, and they were much truer and more fun than those I was performing for in an effort to be popular. But popularity is going to be a big deal to most girls.

Among tween girls, 67 percent say that "having a lot of friends" is among the top three factors that give them confidence. But—here's where it gets tricky—somewhere between the ages of 8 and 12 many girls tend to feel strongly that Mom should not be involved in friendships or help select them:

Want a great way to connect to your daughter and her friends? Why not join more than 10,000 moms who've found American Heritage Girls? It's a nonprofit organization dedicated to the mission of "building women of integrity through service to God, family, community and country." The organization offers badge programs, service projects, girl leadership opportunities, and outdoor experiences to its members. Check it out at ahgonline.org.

AMERICAN HERITAGE GIRLS™

- 67 percent say Mom should never be involved
- 21 percent say "it depends"
- Only 12 percent say Mom should be involved in her friendships and help her select them[3] (thank your daughter today if she's in that small but wise minority!)

This is no small issue to be tackled. The Bible teaches that "His Way" is to walk with wise friends. "He who walks with the wise grows wise, but a companion of fools suffers harm" (Proverbs 13:20). Why is it so critical that you're involved? So that you can teach her during these tween years how to select friends that mirror her values and will stand strong with her in the teen years. The goal is not complete control, but informed guidance. (And if your daughter should come home with notes laced with the language of the drug world and sexual innuendoes, no one is going to stop you from stepping up the level of involvement.) The bottom line is that you need to insert yourself into your daughter's friendships during the tween years, while she is still responsive.

Let me encourage you in two specific ways. Each of these have seemed like burdens to me at times, until I began to look at them as opportunities to research my daughters' sphere of influence. "Make the most of every opportunity" is the admonition of Ephesians 5:16. Girls, it's time to make those carpool moments and slumber-less sleepovers work for you.

Become the Carpool Queen. Driving carpool is a great way to do research on your kids. If you keep the volume on your radio turned down, you can really tune in to the generally unfiltered interaction of friends. You learn who burps loudest, who's the meanest teacher, and who has a boyfriend. Just enjoy and learn. God will guide you in how to use this...ah..."intelligence" later on.

And while it really is the journey and not the destination that counts, you may learn a lot at the destination as well. Sitting on the sidelines of a soccer match or munching on fries at McDonald's with the Bible quiz team just might turn out to be the wisest investment of time a mom can make. After all, it was with my Carpool Queen crown on that I sat at Denny's at midnight, witnessing the shocking conversation of my 14-year-old Lexi and her cussing, sexually open-minded young friend. With the exception of my faithful friend Kim Helsel, I was the only other mom forgoing sleep to carpool that night. I'm so glad I was there. I didn't interfere much with Lexi's gentle but firm defense of abstinence, but I was able to follow up with her later on and encourage her. Be the Carpool Queen!

Become the Sleepover Diva. By this, I really mean that your goal should be to become the hostess with the mostest. You may be hosting a sleepover or a championship bowling celebration party. Whatever the catalyst, make it a goal that your home is *the* home to be at.

In 1988, before Bob and I married, we dreamed about what kind of home we would build. One of our strongest desires was to have a home where all the kids wanted to hang out. Check it off the list! My house is rarely a haven of peace and quiet. With a son in college who lives in our basement, an army of visiting college co-eds, 2 teenage girls, and 65 high-school students that Bob and I have taken under our wings since we started Grace Prep high school, *chaos* better describes my home than does *peace.* But we wouldn't have it any other way.

We *earned* the status of "hangout."

First, we earned it by making our home kid-friendly. In our kids' younger years, we built a really neat pool with a wraparound deck. When our kids were in their tweens, we built a secret room in the attic that you could only get to through the roof in Rob's room. As they approached high school, we refinished our basement and invested in a big-screen TV, and my parents contributed an air-hockey table. Our house is hangout friendly.

Second, we've created opportunities for friends to come to game or movie nights. And these are often game and movie nights on steroids! When *King Kong* was released on DVD, we invited all the older tweens and teens our kids knew over to watch. Our table centerpiece was a huge stuffed monkey with an old Barbie doll—she comes in handy for *something*—in his arms! Banana cream pie, banana splits, banana milkshakes, and banana bread smothered in cream cheese icing were served to meet the theme of the night! Who could resist? (Sometimes we can't get the parents to leave!)

Why are we so creative and vigilant in making our home a fun place? One really obvious reason for this is so we can protect our kids. If your daughter is invited to a sleepover at someone else's house, she just might be watching *SAW I, II, III, IV,* and *V!* She could end up on the internet with unfiltered access, which recently resulted in one of my friends' daughters seeing some mild porn. It's smart to be the host home. So pop the corn and pull out the sleeping bags that will never be used for sleeping. A connecting mom is a Sleepover Diva.

Does that mean your daughter shouldn't ever go to someone else's house for a sleepover? Not really. My girls have and they love it, but we make sure we know and trust the families who are hosting.

Barbara Rainey, cofounder with Dennis Rainey of FamilyLife, encouraged me as I was writing this book by telling me, "I had very strong preferences and did not let my girls go to sleepovers unless we knew the family fairly well. I remember one time calling a mom I didn't know and being really nervous wondering what she'd think of me. I was asking what the girls would be doing, what movie they were going to watch, and who would be there. Even then I was hesitant, knowing the mom could have said all the right things but not really meant them."

You aren't alone here. It's okay to be cautious. My friend Kim, whom

SLeePover Queens GeT TO SHaRe ✝ Jesus

A beautiful benefit is that we get to tell kids about Jesus by showing them his love. According to Child Evangelism Fellowship, 86 percent of people come to know Christ before the age of 15. How great a privilege it is for us to be a part of sharing God's love with kids! While I don't pull out the Bible and preach at kids that come over, I try to make them feel loved and just let them see how we do life with Jesus. For example, we pray before dinner or at bedtime or let them see me reading my Bible in the early morning. If the conversation goes anywhere, I roll with it. Otherwise, I just pray for them and love on them!

I mentioned earlier in the chapter, even has a "no sleepover policy"—something that's becoming more and more common—and her girls are perfectly well-adjusted.

Pray for Your Daughter's Friendships

I don't want you to become paranoid about friendships, but I do want to encourage you that the tween years are the best years to teach your daughter to be discerning about her friendships. Trying to do this in her teen years, when it really counts, will be an uphill climb. Actually, in her late tweens is when the battle becomes intense. That's about the time you are sending her off to middle school, which is what prompted Fern Nichols to ask God for some moms to pray with her so her son would stay free from negative peer pressure, temptations, and troubles he might encounter. Fern found a few friends to pray with and today she's the leader of over 18,000 school prayer groups around the globe, under the name of Moms In Touch International.

"Wherever a child goes to school, they need prayer," says Nichols, age 65. "We are raising our children in very precarious times. For moms to know there is a community of praying moms that will lift up their child's name in faith is bringing great hope to many fearful moms."[4]

Fern emphasizes that our children are in a spiritual battle every day. God desires for them to live a full and abundant life. Satan desires their destruction. The enemy will usually not use blatantly evil encounters to seduce them, but will enter subtly through relationships. That's why we have to be so involved in our daughter's friendships, teaching her to be discerning as she moves toward those years when she will be making decisions with less input from us.

I have never known anyone to pray quite as diligently for her children as my mom does. To this day, she is sensitive to the Lord, who awakens her early with a specific sense of which child or grandchild will need an extra measure of prayer and in what area. Just three weeks ago, I told her I had awakened with an extra burden to pray for my sweet son Rob's future wife. I'm not sure we've met her. If we have, we don't know she's the one yet. But I was on my face with carpet fibers against my face for that precious one. My comment stopped my mom in her tracks. "The Lord awakened me early this morning to pray for her too," she said. Though I don't know where she is, who she is, or what she was experiencing on February 12, 2010, her future mother-in-law and grandmother-in-law were burdened to intercede for her.

What an honor to know that the God of the universe knows far more than we do about our children, no matter what their stage of life, and is eager to hear our heart's desires.

If you're not in a prayer group of some type, why not try Fern Nichols's method of finding a praying mom to join you. Just ask the Lord. Who knows how it might turn out!

Her Way

This chapter is really about examining yourself and the way you interact with your daughter's peers. You have a great chance right now to really think through your family standards about sleepovers. (For example, in our home we allow none on school or church nights.) What are your standards, and how have you communicated them to your daughter—or do you need to do that? How do you just hang out with your daughter's friends, and what should you change so you have more influence? Write your goals and thoughts below.

_____

_____

_____

_____

_____

_____

_____

_____

_____

_____

_____

_____

❀ ❀ ❀ ❀ ❀

Prayer for wisdom and positive peer pressure
based on Proverbs 13:20

*Oh Lord, thank you for being my constant companion and friend. Please let (*insert your daughter's name*) know that she will never have a greater friend than you. During these years when friendship plays such an epic role in her little heart, please surround her with friends who you know will grow up to be positive influencers in her teen years. I pray she would choose to walk with wise friends and that they would grow wise together. Specifically, I pray for (*insert names of daughter's friends*) and ask you to surround them with adults who will steer them toward wise choices. May my daughter never be a companion of fools and suffer the harm of such a choice. In Jesus' Name, amen!*

❀ ❀ ❀ ❀ ❀

Barbara Rainey on BFFs

Dannah: A BFF ("best friend forever") can make or break a moral value system! How can a mom make sure her daughter's friends are providing positive peer pressure to live out values you have placed into her?

Barbara: Dennis and I did a lot of "redirecting"…encouraging some friendships over others. It's easy to do this simply by saying yes to the time your daughter spends with some friends and no to others.

Dannah: Did you ever tell them outright that you thought a friend was bad for them?

Barbara: It can be dicey, as you don't want to be critical of another child or her family. The conversations have to be done wisely and carefully—but yes. We also had more general conversations explaining why certain relationships were healthy and others might not be. We taught our kids to find friends with similar values and convictions. Our favorite verse was "Bad company corrupts good morals."

Dannah: When is the best time to have those kinds of conversations?

Barbara: It's especially important to set those good standards when your kids are tweens or in the early teen years. By the time they are juniors or seniors in high school, your influence is waning and you become more of a coach.

If you have an older tween, you'll want to get them a copy of So You're About to Be a Teenager: Godly Advice for Preteens on Friends, Love, Sex, Faith, and Other Issues. *Barbara and Dennis Rainey wrote it with their children, Rebecca and Samuel, when they were young adults. I consider it essential reading for today's older tween! For more information, go to www.familylife.com.*

"I am seriously concerned about relationships, especially with boys. My eight-year-old daughter, Hannah, has told me that she had three boyfriends this year (in second grade). One boyfriend wanted to kiss her in the hallway, and we had to have a serious discussion about how inappropriate it is for an eight-year-old to have a boyfriend, never mind kissing."

Sheri, mom of Hannah, 8, and Leah, 6
From the conversation at SecretKeeperGirl.com

CHAPTER ELEVEN

Way #6: Dream with Her About Her Prince

I t was New Year's Eve 2002, and my dad had brought the whole family to Sydney, Australia, to see the fireworks that his pyrotechnics system shoots off each year. Since Sydney is the first city on the globe to enter the New Year, it's a big show. I think Bob was climbing the Sydney Harbor Bridge with my dad to wire up some fireworks when it happened.

What?

The big question.

Lexi and I were touring St. Andrews Cathedral with my mom. Enraptured with the large statues, my little nine-year-old girl was running off a string of "why" questions, and I was doing my best to keep up with them. Then she asked the big one.

His Way

"A wife of noble character who can find? She is worth far more than rubies. Her husband has full confidence in her and lacks nothing of value. She brings him good, not harm all the days of her life."

PROVERBS 31:10-12

CORE VALUES: Purity, marriage

"Mommy," she said in her sweet voice. "Why do they call Mary a 'virgin'?"

It wasn't the first time she'd posed the big question. That happened when she was five. She'd jumped off the school bus, propped her hands on her hips, and said, "Mommy, you know those eggs that are in my belly?"

"Yes," I said beginning to ask God for a large vat of wisdom to pour into the conversation.

"Well, I was thinking. How does my body know when it's married to turn them into babies?" she asked as if it were the easiest question in the world to answer.

I quickly ascertained that given my daughter's extra gift of being verbose, I might be giving her entire kindergarten class a lesson if we proceeded. On the other hand, I knew that some children just need to know early. I quickly told the Lord that I'd leave it in his hands and started to give her an honest answer.

"Well," I said. "Sometimes when a husband and wife want to show each other how very much they love each other, they hold each other very tightly."

I was going to go on, but Lexi jumped in delight and said, "I knew it was something just like that." And off she went.

I thought I might get the Mother of the Universe Award right then and there, but it was not to be.

The next day she got off the bus in tears. Why? Uncle Darin had visited her at kindergarten and he had hugged her and it was "really tight." It took me some time to calm my child and convince her she wasn't pregnant. I explained to her that I hadn't told her all the details the day before and that I was sorry. This came with a promise to tell her everything when it was time.

It wasn't yet.

A mother knows.

But that day at St. Andrews Cathedral, in Sydney, Australia, it was.

"I'm going to tell you, Lexi," I said. "It's kind of a big deal, and I'd like to tell you when we're all alone—so can we do it later in our room?"

"Yep," she said and ran off to look at the next statue.

Talking to your daughter about God's beautiful gift of sex isn't easy. The world's casual crushing and complete destruction of its meaning has made it difficult. And it's gotten so we have to start earlier and earlier because our little girls are being pressed earlier and earlier to have boyfriends. I have to hold myself back every time a white-haired grandma leans toward her pigtailed granddaughter and teasingly asks her, "So, do you have a boyfriend?" This question, usually asked with a chuckle and a batting of the eyes, is generally meant to be just silly conversation, but I know too much to consider it cute. It's dangerous.

Keep Her Off the Boy-Crazy Train

Being in a dating relationship for six months or longer is a significant risk factor for early teen sexual activity. Can you see why it might not be "cute" for our 8-to-12-year-olds to be boy-crazy or to have multiple boyfriends while they are still in the fourth grade? If your daughter develops the pattern of "needing" a guy when she's eight or nine, she's going to be in many six-month relationships in her teen years. That's not wise. Let's help her stay off the boy-crazy train.

Approximately 50 percent of 16-year-old girls are sexually active, and an overwhelming percentage are boy-crazy. In the survey of 1200 Christian teens that was conducted to write *Lies Young Women Believe,* I was heartbroken to find out just how dependent Christian girls are on guys. It didn't matter what school type—public, private, or home—68 percent of Christian girls said they'd be happier if they had a boyfriend. There was no other lie we uncovered that was so prevalent among all three school environments. It doesn't matter how you're choosing to educate your girl—when she's in high school she's at risk to feel a pull to *"need"* a guy.

This hasn't happened with my two girls. With Autumn, whom I've had for only two years, I attribute it to the gentler and less sexual Chinese culture she grew up in. (Recently she was listening to some Chinese rap and I was worried. When I inquired about the lyrics, I found out it was a song about "listening to your mom"!) With Lexi, I feel like it's due to a lot of prayer and putting into place the wise plans of parents who have gone before me, like Tim and Beverly LaHaye, who wrote the parenting handbook I used in talking to my kids about sex, *Raising Sexually Pure Kids*.[1]

Here's the challenge: You want to keep her off the boy-crazy train while at the very same time developing within her a love for marriage. How do you do this? You do it by being positive about boys and telling her about what she can have in the future—not by being paranoid about boys and telling her what she can't have now. Dream with her about the pure relationship God wants her to have one day, and teach her that the beauty of that relationship depends on how she lives today.

Our "His Way" verse for this chapter says,

✳ ✳ ✳

"A wife of noble character who can find? She is worth far more than rubies. Her husband has full confidence in her and lacks nothing of value. She brings him good, not harm, all the days of her life" (Proverbs 31:10-12).

✳ ✳ ✳

The verse is clear that a wife is good "all the days of her life." The days your daughter lives when she's 8, 12, or 16 are spoken of in these verses. As a mom who wants to pass on a biblical view of marriage, I use this verse to remind me that every day is a day to tell my girls how great it will be to marry the man of their dreams one day, and to encourage them to make choices that "do him good" today. That may mean not being boy-crazy when she's 8, or giving her heart away to guys when she's 13, or giving her body away when she's 16.

How do you talk to your daughter about saving herself when she's still so little? Here are a couple of important things to consider.

Positive messages are more potent than negative messages. Don't get obsessed with dissing boy-craziness every time you see it or hear about it. Focus instead on positive conversations about your daughter's future husband. My favorite tool to stimulate these kinds of conversations during the tween years is *The Princess and The Kiss* by Jennie Bishop. I gave Lexi a copy on her ninth birthday, but you could give it to your daughter when she's even younger. The story of a princess who is saving her prized possession—her first kiss—for the man she will marry is sweet and opens up conversations about the future in an age-appropriate way.

You do have to address the issue of boy-craziness directly from time to time, of course—but do it with questions, *not statements.* In an effort to keep your statements positive, let me remind you once again about the power of a question. Any kind of open-ended question will do. I asked questions about boys when we were watching television. ("Gee, I wonder why so many of these shows for girls your age are about boys. What do you think of that?") I asked questions when she told me her friends had boyfriends. (Lexi: "Mom, two of my friends at school have boyfriends." Me: "What do you think of that?") I asked questions when girls started chasing big brother, Rob, in middle school. ("Lexi, there are some girls at school who like Robby. What do you think of that?")

Let me remind you that asking her questions is a form of developing moral values by induction. I ask her questions to know how she feels about herself and the world, and then I get to respond to those emotions and direct them with more questions.

Establishing a vision for saving herself for marriage, and delaying the boy-craziness, is a critical tool to protect your daughter's purity. But eventually, "everyone" will have a boyfriend. Though that may not happen until she's 14, it's time to get ready for it when she's 8!

Introduce Your Family Standards About Dating When She's a Tween

I recently worked with a mom who was distraught that her son was "dating" a girl in middle school. I first asked her how old she'd hoped he'd be before he dated, and she said, "16." Then, I asked her when she'd ever talked to her son about that. She just looked at me, puzzled.

"Well, he's only in seventh grade," she said. "It wasn't time to talk about it yet."

"Obviously it was," I said.

By the time a girl is 11, 30 percent of her peers will have had a boyfriend.[2] Since this drive to be in a relationship only escalates, it's important to talk to your daughter before it happens.

At some point, you have to tell your kids point-blank what your standards are. We adopted the dating protocol of the LaHayes after reading their book.

Our teenagers are allowed to go on group dates for special events as soon as they hit high school. That means they could go with a date to a chaperoned formal event, if they wanted, at the age of 14 or 15. Rob took advantage of this. Lexi did not. The first boy asked her by writing it on a piece of paper and whacking her in the head with it. The second one had already asked her friend. So, she decided to dress to the nines with five other girls and take public transportation to her first formal. She had a blast without any guys. Autumn will have her chance to decide how to approach it this year.

I believe the LaHayes are correct in pinpointing the fact that curiosity is dampened by this open opportunity to take the next step in guy–girl interaction. Though we've navigated a few attractions, none of our teenagers have yet chosen to pursue dating relationships during high school.

REACHING OUT FOR HEALING

If you are a married woman, I recommend reading *Pursuing the Pearl: The Quest for a Pure and Passionate Marriage*. It's a book I wrote chronicling my healing, and it offers specific advice on how to pursue your own healing. But you don't need my story to heal. Reach out to those around you in your own church community for the healing. It's all around you. In fact, you won't believe where you'll find it if you just start to reach out!

Our teenagers are allowed to go on single dates when they are 16, as long as we are actively involved in the planning and execution of the evening. What do I mean by actively involved? Well, Lexi and Autumn know that any guy who wants to take them out has to go through an interview with their dad. Period. Non-negotiable. If the boy seems to have honorable intentions and is someone we feel comfortable with, we'll most likely allow them to spend a carefully planned, very public evening together. We'll be approving everything they do, and they'll be in close contact with us. That's what I mean by involved.

Frankly, they aren't that interested in this opportunity yet. Both of the girls are into that 16-year-old freedom, and they are too involved in acting, soccer, basketball, and voice lessons to be interested in guys. (They now attend Grace Prep, a high school my husband founded, where we try to instill similar values into the students, and that helps them to have positive peer pressure to live this standard out!)

As for Rob, he had to call the father of any girl he wanted to take out. (And did so when he took girls to formals, but he never felt led to take anyone on a date outside of a formal event.)

Finally, we've discouraged them from being in any exclusive relationships until they are out of high school. We really want them to enjoy high school free from any of the drama relationships can bring, and we don't want their hearts to be wounded by excessive relationships. Maybe you, like me, know something about that. One mom on my secretkeepergirl .com blog commented,

❈ ❈ ❈

"Date...break up...next...date...break up...next...and so on. It seems to me that each one took a little piece of my heart and now my hurts and mistakes follow me through adulthood. I wish someone had explained to me how this disposable view of relationships is wrong and saddens God."

—Joy, Cleveland, Ohio

❈ ❈ ❈

A disposable view of relationships is exactly what we did not want our teenagers to experience firsthand. So we began to introduce our standards to them when they were nine in an effort to keep them off the boy- or girl-crazy trains during their teen years, and it seems to have worked. (Remember, we were just following the advice of wiser parents. We didn't make this stuff up!)

I can't overstate the importance of communicating these standards when your daughter is a tween, even if that seems difficult. I also can't understate how easy it is. My kids' hearts were so innocent that it was just comfortable and natural to discuss. Both Rob and Lexi were like, "Well, okay! If that's how it works." Autumn has had a much harder time understanding our values. She did not grow up hearing "wait" during her own value-formation years. Though in a more modest culture, she was exposed to boyfriend–girlfriend relationships at a young age and is a little uncomfortable with our desire that she wait. What I'm trying to say is that it's easy to establish this standard if you do it before the hormones kick in and "everyone else" has a boyfriend. If you wait, you may find yourself working a lot harder.

Have the Big Talk About Sex *Before* She Turns Ten

We've already concluded that moral values are formed during these critical tween years. Since some of the most life-impacting values are in the sexual arena, I'm afraid you're actually going to have to have the big sex talk now—the one that so many parents think can wait until their children are 11 or 12.

I've read the work of just about every Christian psychologist or family expert out there, and they all agree that this talk needs to take place much earlier than we, as parents, are generally comfortable having it. Dr. James Dobson, for example, says, "Sometime between six and nine, depending on maturity and interest of an individual (and what is being heard in the neighborhood), he or she ought to understand how conception occurs."[3] What happens if you wait? Jimmy Hester, founder of True Love Waits and editor of the biblically based Christian Sex Education curriculum says,

························· ❊ ❊ ❊ ·························

"By ten or eleven years, many children who have not received adequate instructions about the facts of sexuality become disturbed and worry about what is real. They usually have heard bits and pieces of facts from peers."[4]

························· ❊ ❊ ❊ ·························

Talking to your children about sex between the ages of six and ten isn't a moral choice, it's a strategic choice. It is much easier to build a sexual value system from the ground up than to dismantle untruths and rebuild. Take a deep breath. In the next few paragraphs, I might stretch you right out of your comfort zone with words like *vagina, penis,* and *intercourse.* These are all words you need to actually use with your daughter before she's ten years old. (As my husband usually says to parents when he's doing our presentation called "Raising Sexually Pure Kids," "You made 'em. I think you know how this works!")

Be prepared to answer questions. The good news is that most times your kids will ask when they are ready to hear the basic mechanics of sexuality. If they are under the age of six (like Lexi was when she asked about the "eggs in her belly"), proceed carefully but truthfully. At this age, they are generally not developmentally ready for a brief lesson in conception, but you can answer them by explaining that "a husband and wife often want to show each other how very much they love each other. When they do this, they hold each other in a special way, and I'd like to tell you about that when you're a little older." From there, the conversation should flow into things they *are* ready for, such as where the baby grows. For example, "After they hold each other in this very special way, a baby often begins to grow inside of the momma! It's a very exciting time for a family."

If your child is over the age of six, it's time to dive in with those scary real words!

Be accurate and explicit. While I do not want you to be indiscreet or crude, it is important that you explain the simple facts using real words. You might say something like, "When a husband and wife want to show each other how very much they love each other, they use a gift God gave to them that's called sex. They are all alone, and they are naked. God tells us that there is no need to cover their bodies when they are married, and that they can enjoy hugging and touching each other. During this time, they hold each other very closely, and the husband can fit his penis into the wife's vagina. This act is God's special way to get the sperm from the man into the woman so the eggs in her body can be fertilized. This is called intercourse. That's how babies are made."

With our son, Rob, my husband had this simple conversation without any tools. And with me in the next room listening and praying. Imagine my momentary fear when I overheard the strange beginning of their big talk:

❈ ❈ ❈

Bob: Robby, I want to tell you about sex. Do you know about sex?

Rob: Yes. I do.

Bob: Where did you learn about it?

Rob: On the internet.

(Me gulping and moving toward a mild momentary mom freak-out fit!)

Bob: What do you mean by that?

Rob: Well, sometimes when I play games on the internet it says, "Sex: male or female?" So I know about that, Dad.

(Me in the next room: *Whew!*)

Bob: Well, that's how the word *sex* is used as a noun. I'm going to tell you how it's used as a verb.

❈ ❈ ❈

That's my man for ya. Cool as a cuke.

If you want to be the continuing expert on sex for your daughter in the years to come, be positive. If I have a pet peeve about how Christian parents approach sex education it's this one word: *negativity*! Sex is a great gift from God, and when it is not misused, it is not only pleasurable but holy! Filling our kids with a negative "don't-have-sex" message is a horrible strategy. When they are puzzled by desires as teens or new questions come up, they won't come to *you* to ask for the answers. They'll turn to sources who have not treated sex as taboo.

Remember, this big talk is only the beginning. For the next 10 to 12 years, you'll be helping your kids live out their sexual values and develop a more complete theology about marriage, sex, and family. When they're teens, it will be your great honor to introduce more about sex if you've kept the door of communication open. At that time, you can talk about pleasure, parenting, emotional intimacy, and how marriage is a beautiful picture of Christ and the church. There is so much good stuff to share.

FOR a CONNECTING mom's TOOLBOX

Being fully healed from any sexual sin in your past and free from any current addiction or pattern is a really important step to ready yourself to introduce a healthy view of sexuality to your daughter. Here are a few great resources for your journey:

- *Pursuing the Pearl: The Quest for a Pure, Passionate Marriage* by Dannah Gresh, which I mentioned previously, is great if you've got some sexual sin in your past and you're looking for healing.

- *When Godly People Do Ungodly Things* by Beth Moore is a thrilling scriptural look at how to overcome the seduction of our culture, and it helps you understand why if you've already fallen for it.

- *Finding Grace* by Donna Van-Liere is the memoir of my *New York Times* bestselling friend who candidly shares how she overcame childhood sexual abuse and other challenges.

How can you be positive now? By communicating the truth that sex is a great gift for a husband and wife, even if your own heart has been crushed by sexual sin. God's word, not our experience, is the standard of truth. And he says that sex is good. Adam and Eve were naked and not ashamed!

If you do feel some shame, I urge you to start the process of healing. God confronted me with the need to heal sexually when Lexi was still a baby. I learned that in order for me be a good mentor in the area of sexuality and purity, I was going to have to take my mask of secrecy off and confess my sin within safe relationships so I could heal.

Give Her a Symbol of Purity

When Lexi was just five years old, Bob came home with a special heart-shaped box. The inside of the lid was engraved, "To Lexi. From Daddy. Something Blue. December 28, 1998." The box contained a simple blue gemstone bracelet that Lexi can carry or wear on her wedding day. It was the beginning of a precious collection of hope.

For her tenth birthday, we added an antique necklace. Inside a simple heart hanging on the silver chain is a cluster of diamond chips from her great-grandmother's original diamond engagement ring. It was "something old."

By the time Lexi was 16, she had a brand-new sister. She and Autumn each got a specially made handkerchief designed by their Grammy Barker (my mom), and presented in special boxes selected by their Mom-Mom Gresh. Made from brand-new white Irish linen and trimmed with handmade tatting by the girls' great-Aunt Vale, it is "something new."

You see the plan. We are dreaming with them. And pointing them toward a decision for purity that ultimately only they can make. A symbol of the conversations you've had and any special decisions they've made is a great tool to keep reminding them of the gift that's ahead. Through the years I've heard of so many great ideas for gifts you can give your daughter as a symbol of her purity. You can give her a ring on her twelfth birthday. A gold key to wear around her neck can represent the key to her heart to be given to her husband. My son has a "certificate of purity" that he and his dad signed at J.H. Ranch when Rob was in eighth grade.

Be creative and ask God to guide your process, but consider giving your daughter a special symbol of her purity.

Is your daughter boy-crazy? If so, how can you change that ever so gently so you achieve success in changing her heart? What are your family dating standards? If you don't know, when can you discuss them with your husband (or your daughter's dad, if you are a single mom or divorced)? Knowing these standards is so critical to being able to communicate them effectively. Consider where your daughter is in her readiness to hear about God's gift of sex, and make a plan to discuss it with her in the right time. Take note of any special ideas you thought of as you read this chapter so you can follow through with them in the near future!

_____

_____

_____

_____

_____

_____

_____

_____

_____

_____

❊ ❊ ❊ ❊ ❊

Prayer for purity and marriage
based on Proverbs 31:10-12

Oh heavenly Father! Thank you for the beautiful gifts of purity and marriage. May (insert your daughter's name) grow to treasure them. May she desire to be a wife of noble character—which becomes more and more difficult to find in a society that doesn't value marriage and motherhood. May her one-day husband have confidence in her because she has lived her life so well. May she do her future husband good every single day of her life, including today. Help me to heal from any hurt in my past so I can be a good role model and mentor for her as she thinks about marriage and purity. In a world where Satan is so successful at devouring our children with sexuality and sin, I declare that he will not have my daughter! In Jesus' Name, amen!

❊ ❊ ❊ ❊ ❊

GINGER GARRETT on BOY-craziness

Dannah: Ginger, your daughters are tweens. What's one way you keep them off the "boy-crazy train"?

Ginger: A word they hear a lot from me is "appropriate." They are learning that just as their life will have stages, true love will have stages. What is appropriate for a woman within marriage is not appropriate for a pre-teen with a crush. The word "appropriate" communicates wisdom without burdening them with shame. Sexuality isn't wrong, but it can be inappropriate.

Dannah: I love that! How are you working to prepare them for a time when it's "appropriate" for them to date?

Ginger: My girls love for my husband to take them on "dates." He invests in their precious lives by devoting an evening just to them, to listen, encourage, and counsel. The girls know what it is like to be honored and treated as a godly daughter of Christ. I appreciate having my daughters associate "dates" with evenings that honor and encourage them.

Dannah: That's a great way to train your girls to expect to be honored by any guy who wants to date them in the future. If a mom doesn't have a husband who can provide an experience like this, a grandfather or even an older brother or uncle can do the same thing!

A great resource for mother–daughter bonding is Ginger's nonfiction book Beauty Secrets of the Bible. *A secretkeeper girl.com blogging mom clued me in to this fantastic book, as she's used it to have beauty nights with her tween girls! For more information, go to gingergarrett.com.*

"My daughter has a real enemy in Satan himself and our culture (and even some of our churches play him down as a joke!). He is constantly trying to manipulate her thinking, wound her emotionally, and scar her and thus prevent her from having a close relationship with her heavenly Father. Having her know who she is in Christ is my number-one goal before she leaves my home and the ONE thing I see being attacked on every level EVERY day. This is spiritual warfare!"

Kisha
From the conversation at SecretKeeperGirl.com

CHAPTER 12

A Connecting Mom
Is Not a Perfect Mom

I couldn't believe it. Moments ago I'd been sitting at the kitchen table ready to sink my teeth into a huge plate of PMS magic—cheese-stuffed meat loaf glazed with barbecue sauce, mashed potatoes, corn, and a freshly baked blueberry muffin! It had been an extra stressful week, and I was beyond tired. Somewhere between "amen" and my first bite, Bob casually asked me about—brace yourself—the laundry! Now, in *his* defense, I think he was wondering whether he needed to do it. It seemed to be stacked as high as Mt. Everest.

It was a neutral comment to him. *But* I hate doing laundry. And I was tired. And I had my mind on ten minutes of calorie consumption to soothe my stress. (Did I mention PMS?)

I lost it big time.

Before I'd had time to consider my actions, I'd flipped my plate into the air and was watching it soar toward my husband in slow-mo. I imme-diately wanted to take it back, but it was too late. Just about the time the meat loaf cleared Bob's left shoulder and the mashed potatoes landed with a thump on the table, I burst into tears. Lexi, my precious little girl, just sat staring at me with her eyes wide as saucers. Rob, a middle-schooler at the time, was trying to hold back a smirk. I'd surely just scarred my children for life. I scampered off to my bedroom, holding back tears.

Had I actually just thrown a plate of meat loaf and mashed potatoes at my husband?

What happened next is the stuff that years of counseling, couple mentoring, and marriage seminars are made of—and Bob and I have had it all! My husband calmly followed me to our bedroom. He pulled my hands from my teary eyes and looked into them with a playful smile.

"Honey, we have two choices," he said. "We can stay here and hide and make this a horrible memory for our kids, or we can go down there and turn it into one of the most hilarious moments ever. I'm game for number two. What do you think?"

Through my tears, I followed him as he took me downstairs by the hand. He guided me quietly to my spot. Lexi was still wide-eyed, and Rob was still smirking. I meekly apologized. Then my husband began a comedy routine that to this day I say deserves a date on Leno. He was at his best when I was at my worst. Before long, everyone was laughing about mom's terribly inaccurate meat-loaf spiral.

"Do you want another plate of mashed potatoes and meat loaf?" asked my sweet little girl through her laughter. "I'll get it for you as long as you don't throw it at me!"

If you hadn't figured it out already, I'm not a perfect mom. My kids aren't perfect kids. The Gresh family is not the model family. We *are* a family who puts the fun in dysFUNctional. We've learned to laugh at our failures and pick up the pieces for each other with a lighthearted sense of forgiveness.

But we aren't perfect.

And…

Writing this book has made me realize how lax Bob and I have become with media limits.

Lately, I've been working too much.

My girls often stretch the limits on modesty.

I still get PMS!

As I sit here finishing a book that encourages you to keep the little in your girl so she can be a pure and whole teenage girl, I still have a few years left until my precious 16-year-old girls are out of my home and demonstrating they've embraced all the values I've poured into and prayed over them.

I'm still in this with you.

And truth be told, though I'm on the right track, I don't know how it's going to turn out. Sometimes that scares me.

The Good News: Prayer!

I could not imagine raising my children without the wonderful tool of prayer. It's the number-one thing to put in your connecting mom toolbox. And yet—get ready for yet another confession—I don't consider myself to be the prayer warrior that some of my friends seem to be. So for this tool I've turned to the best of the best in the discipline of prayer: the founder of Moms In Touch International, Fern Nichols. If you're unfamiliar with Moms In Touch, it's a prayer network of tens of thousands of moms who pray regularly for their children and the schools they attend. There are groups in all 50 states and in over 140 countries. I'm in the Moms In Touch prayer group at Grace Prep.

I recently caught up with Fern—who is a few years ahead of you and me in parenting—to ask about an area where nothing but prayer could ultimately control the outcome: her adult daughter's husband. I asked her if she had been praying for this godly man when her daughter, Trisha, was a tween.

"Actually, I prayed for her spouse from birth," answered Fern. And she never ran out of prayers to pray, either. Why? Because she turned to the Scriptures to inform and shape her prayers, which is what she trains other moms to do as they pray for their children together at Moms In Touch meetings. Just lean in and see if this doesn't inspire you to reach for your Bible the next time you pray for your daughter.

"Knowing that the Word of God was his will, I prayed in faith," continued Fern. "Here are a few of the prayers I prayed on a regular basis. I asked God that she would not be 'unequally yoked' with an unbeliever (2 Corinthians 6:14). That her husband would love the Lord with all his heart, soul, mind, and strength, and his neighbor as himself (Matthew 22:37-38). I prayed that God would prepare her heart to be a 'helpmate' to her husband and that her future husband would 'love her just as Christ loved the church' (Ephesians 5:22-33). And that together they would serve and bring glory to the Lord (Joshua 24:15)."

Did the prayers work?

Oh, yes!

"I love telling the story of her husband," affirmed Fern. "It truly is a witness to the promise of Jeremiah 33:3, which says that if we call to him, he will answer. There were two guy friends that Trisha hung out with her freshman year in high school. They were not Christians, but they were wonderful, kind, moral young men. My daughter and I prayed for their salvation often, as did the moms in my Moms In Touch group. There was a 'Harvest Crusade' that my daughter asked if I would drive them to. At the crusade both of the young men accepted Christ

FINISH WITH a PARTY!

Here's a little bit of tween girl-time fun from my *Mother/Daughter Devos* book. It's an appropriate "be with her" activity to end on. It'll make any connecting mom's worries melt away (even if you've just thrown a meat-loaf spiral!).

Melted chocolate chocolate-chip cookie dough pops!

1 batch of your favorite chocolate-chip cookie dough

2 Hershey chocolate bars

toothpicks

Grab your little girl and have a blast rolling the chocolate-chip cookie dough into little balls and pressing a toothpick into the center of each one. Freeze them!

When they are frozen, grab your little girl again and dip each ball into freshly melted chocolate bars.

Have a girls' frozen chocolate-chip cookie dough pop party!

as their Savior. Nine years later, my daughter married one of them—Chris. He is a godly man who loves my daughter. They are active in their church and are intentional about raising their two children to love the Lord. Words cannot express my joy in his being part of our family."

Chris himself recognizes that it was Fern's prayers that shaped him. In a recent e-mail to her about this book, he said, "When I am reminded of how much you prayed for Trisha's future spouse, I just know that God was answering and working those prayers out in my life with the promise of getting me ready to love and lead your beautiful daughter."

My heart is overwhelmed at the thought that my prayers could do this for my sweet Autumn and my precious Lexi. For ultimately, the reason we are protecting our girls and giving them every opportunity to remain "little" for as long as they deserve is so they can grow up to be adult women in healthy, happy marriages who are raising children to love the Lord—and living the rest of their lives in glorious testimony to his goodness, no matter what the call on their lives may be.

Depend on the God Who Builds and Repairs

I have a long way to go until I can be sure I have the satisfaction of knowing that my children have fully embraced my value system. So I keep on plugging away, realizing more and more each day that it all comes down to prayer for this imperfect family of mine! At the example of women like Fern, I've turned to the Scriptures to guide my prayers. I am particularly comforted by Psalm 127:1:

························· ❃ ❃ ❃ ·························

"Unless the LORD builds the house,
its builders labor in vain."

························· ❃ ❃ ❃ ·························

You know that famous chapter in the Bible that mentions a big ol' quiver full of kids being a blessing? Well, this verse is the first one in that chapter. So get this…while God has charged me to raise these kids to love him, ultimately I am not the one building this house. And it's not my husband, Bob, either. It's God!

In fact, for those of us who have a few too many things to confess, it's even better than that! The Hebrew word for "build" actually means "repair." *"Unless the Lord repairs the house, its builders labor in vain."* I don't know about you, but this house has needed a lot of repairs. And I'm not talking about the Maytag clothes washer I've been praying through "just one more load" these past few weeks. (I've been assured that since it sounds like a 747 about to take off when it spins, it's got only a few loads left!)

No, it's been my heart that has needed repairs. Bob's heart has needed repairs. And—oh God, help us—our precious children have needed their hearts to be repaired. It really seems to me that if we spend all our time doing, doing, doing for our family and never praying, praying, praying… our efforts may very well be in vain. So I claim this prayer as mine (and am happy to loan it out to you):

※ ※ ※

"Lord, build and repair the Gresh home heart by heart. Build and repair me. Build and repair Bob. Build and repair Rob, Lexi, and Autumn. Do not let my labor as a mom be in vain!"

※ ※ ※

Whatever your circumstances as you read this, be assured that God makes house calls that are so thorough and complete that the ever-so-lonely Maytag guy looks like a bumbling idiot. God can fix houses. And hearts. Reach out to him if there is something that needs to be fixed. (I'll be asking him to repair the Greshes' broken media-filtering system. Begging him to open hearts as we reclaim old limits and establish a few new ones.) It's okay to be a little broken, as long as you roll up your sleeves to cooperate with God as he builds and repairs again and again.

As you labor to keep the "little" in your girl, don't let it be in vain. Stay in touch with the Lord, be obedient to his nudges in your spirit, and pray the Word of God over your kids as much as you can!

I pray that you would experience no sense of condemnation for how you have chosen to parent, but rather a new sense of direction and hope. I trust that you now have a few more tools to answer the "why's" of parenting "His Way," rather than the world's way. You should be better able to answer your little girl's "why's" so you can instill a biblical moral value system into her heart. Most of all, I hope you'll rely on God to do all the "building" and "repairing."

---

a connecting mom u may know

Fern NICHOLS on PraYING

Dannah: Fern, what's an important tip for praying successfully for our children, especially in the area of purity and their future marriage and children?

Fern: I used Scripture to formulate my prayers.

Dannah: I've shared some of them in the book already. Are there any other scriptures you used for that specific issue?

Fern: That her husband would love her as long as they lived (Matthew 19:5-6). That he would keep himself pure for her before and after the wedding (1 Corinthians 6:18-20). That he would be able to support his family with honor (1 Timothy 6:6-10). That if God blessed him with children he would be a godly dad (Ephesians 6:4).

Dannah: It's really just a matter of finding verses that speak to that part of your daughter's life and adapting them into a prayer for her, right?

Fern: Yes!

Dannah: Did you ever talk to her about what you were praying for her?

Fern: I was intentional to take opportunities to share what God said in his Word about dating relationships. I emphasized on many occasions that God's desire was for her happiness and well-being. Something I shared often was that "obedience brings blessing" and that keeping herself for a godly man would be worth the wait. Together we memorized Psalm 1, which outlined who a blessed (happy) person was. And to this day, as a happily married woman with two children who are growing in their love for the Lord, she can quote almost the whole passage!

Dannah: For those of us who are still waiting and praying, were there ever times when you worried if she'd hear your wisdom and cooperate with your prayers?

Fern: Praying with other moms in Moms In Touch gave me hope and peace during those times when I wasn't sure where she stood. I'm sure she was crazy over some boys, but she wasn't on that "train" long.

If you like the idea of praying Scripture for your tween daughter (and your other children), pick up a copy of Fern's Every Child Needs a Praying Mom. *For more information, go to momsintouch.org.*

Six People Who Kept the Sane in *This* Girl

This is my fifteenth book. For some reason, I'm asked a lot about the number of books I've written, but I've never counted. Until now.

If I've learned anything, it is this: Books are not written alone. They are a collaboration. The team that creates them is made up mostly of servants who don't get their name on the cover, but sweat just about as much as the person who does. To bring that into perspective, let me tell you that I'm writing this from a plane headed to sunny spots in the South, where I intend to sleep in and then take naps in the sun all day while several of the folks below are picking up the baton to bring this book to press. Can't even begin to tell you how much love I have in my heart for them at this moment. Indulge me while I tell you about it. My euphoric just-met-a-deadline-and-on-my-way-to-the-Florida-Keys-love goes out to…

My daughters…Lexi Gresh, who is sitting beside me editing every word I write! (Literally…and telling me she can't help it because she's stuck beside me in a plane with nothing to do.) In some ways, I wish I weren't writing so many of our treasured moments together out on paper for everyone to read, because they are sacred. (I'm glad there are so many millions of moments that are our secrets and no one else's.) However, thanks for being willing to share your life with others. I'm so proud of the fact that you have a transparent heart that's completely anchored in Christ. I know that some of the more recent years have been hard and we've occasionally forgotten how much we like each other, but overall we are enjoying a great relationship. *Autumn Gresh,* who is snoring between the two big guys in my life one row behind me. You had no idea what you were in for on our "gotcha day" two and half years ago, but I think God custom-made you for our family's insane sense of humor and call to be transparent. Thanks for being my daughter.

Harvest House Publishers…Carolyn McCready, who was the last person I spoke to from the airport in Philadelphia. I got right off the phone and told Bob that you're a most supportive editor. You have been patient and have risen up to fill in all my weaknesses and the gaps in the book. I'm honored to call you my new friend. *Paul Gossard* stepped in to make sure the work Carolyn and I did crossed the finish line on time and with excellence. Thanks, Paul, for the hard work and the great encouragement as you raise your little girl! Also *LaRae Weikert, Terry Glaspey, and Bob Hawkins Jr.* for welcoming me into the Harvest House Publishers family with an extra dose of love. Can't wait to come back out to the great Northwest for another visit to one of the most beautiful places in our country.

The Resource Agency…Mike Keil, who was the missing part of our ministry team until a year ago. Bob and I can't remember doing all of this without you. You have taken us to a new level of ministry in just 12 months. I love that you are able to be the administrative front man while Bob goes off on creative tangents and I press into the meat and content of the messages God puts on my heart. Together, we are a complete package.

My Secret Keeper Girl team…Eileen King, who is not only my dear friend watching my back with prayer but also my vigilant assistant. Thanks for keeping me in the right place at the right time while my brain was "doing too much" these past few months. *Melanie Cherland,* my Secret Keeper Girl intern, who is picking up the baton with Carolyn to write some of the content of my fall Harvest House releases so I can take a break.

*Bob Gresh…*who is the man who envisioned a ministry to rescue the hearts of little girls before the enemy even had a swipe at them. You were hearing from God when you prompted me to start Secret Keeper Girl. Last year alone approximately 600 little girls came to know Jesus at our events, tens of thousands were strengthened to pursue purity and modesty, one little girl started the journey of healing from sexual abuse, another led her momma to Jesus after receiving him herself at a Secret Keeper Girl event… just a week before her momma went home to be with him in heaven after a battle with cancer. Those are big moments. And this is your work. I'm honored to help you with it.

*Jesus…*for rescuing me so I can help you rescue others.

Dannah Gresh
March 6, 2010

Notes

Chapter One—A Mom's Greatest Compliment

1. www.apa.org/pi/wpo/sexualizationrep.pdf, retrieved February 2, 2010. This is a report that I will refer to often within the book. I've been analyzing the results of it since 2007 when it was released. If there is one resource cited in my end notes that you should look up, this is it. Everything you need to know about how the culture is damaging our little girls sexually is right here in black and white!

Chapter Two—A Mom's Greatest Fears

1. Haishan Fu, Jacqueline E. Darroch, Taylor Haas, and Nalini Ranjit, "Contraception Failure Rates: New Estimates From the 1995 National Survey of Family Growth," *Family Planning Perspectives* (March/April 1999): 31 (2).

2. Juliet B. Schor, *Born to Buy* (New York: Scribner, 2004), 13.

3. *Good Housekeeping,* August 1, 2006.

4. *Washington Post,* February 20, 2007.

5. Centers for Disease Control and Prevention, J. A. Grunbaum, L. Kann, S.A. Kinchen, et al., "Youth Risk Behavior Surveillance—United States 2001," *Morbidity and Mortality Weekly Report:* "Surveillance Summary" 51, no. 4 (2002).

6. Liz Brody, "Mothers & Daughters Talk About Sex: The *O/Seventeen* Sex Survey," *Oprah* magazine, May 2009, www.oprah.com/printarticlefull/omagazine/200905 -omag-sex-survey, retrieved 6/9/09.

7. Cheryl Wetzstein, "Youthful Indiscretion: Tweens' pairing up worrisome," the *Washington Times,* February 27, 2008, www.highbeam.com/DocPrintaspx?DocId =1g1:175463078, retrieved 9/26/08.

8. Deborah Swaney, "Fast Times: When did 7 become the new 16?" *Family Circle,* November 29, 2008, 48.

9. Marian Merritt, "10-Year-Old Tweens Are Sexting, Study Reports," community .norton.com, 4/21/2009, retrieved 3/3/2010.

10. Joe Kelly, *Dads and Daughters* (New York: Broadway Books, 2002), 38.

Chapter Four—Why Connecting Matters

1. Amanda Onion, "Parent-Child Connection Shapes Brain" abcNEWS.com, December 5, 2005.

2. Joe S. McIlhaney Jr. and Freda McKissic Bush, *Hooked: New Science on How Casual Sex Is Affecting Our Children* (Chicago: Northfield Publishing, 2008), 53.

3. McIlhaney and McKissic, 51.

Chapter Five—How Connecting Forms Values

1. Blaise Pascal, *Pensées and the Provincial Letters* (Mineola, NY: Dover Publications, 2004), pensée 205.

Chapter Six—Way #1: Give Her the Right Dolls to Play With

1. Diane Levin, PhD, "Buy, Buy Childhood: Helping Children Resist the Lure of Today's Media and Commercial Culture," *Early Childhood: The Newsletter of the Winnetka Alliance for Early Childhood,* Spring/Summer 2008, 4.

2. Alix Spiegel, "Old Fashioned Play Builds Serious Skills," npr.org, October 10, 2008, www.npr.org/templates/story/story.php?storyId+19212514, retrieved 10/10/08.

3. Spiegel.

4. Susan Linn, *Consuming Kids* (New York: Anchor, 2004), 61.

5. Deborah Swaney, "Fast Times: When Did 7 Become the New 16?" *Family Circle,* November 29, 2008, 48.

Chapter Seven—Way #2: Celebrate Her Body by Punctuating Her Period

1. Catherine M. Gordon, ed., *The Menstrual Cycle and Adolescent Health,* (Boston: New York Academy of Sciences, 2008), quoted from the article entitled "Pubertal Development and Menarche" by Sara A. DiVall and Sally Radovick.

Chapter Eight—Way #3: Unplug Her from a Plugged-In World

1. Jim Taylor, PhD, *Your Children Under Attack: How Popular Culture Is Destroying*

Your Kids' Values, and How You Can Protect Them (Naperville, IL: Sourcebooks, Inc., 2005), 19.

2. Juliet B. Schor, *Born to Buy* (New York: Scribner, 2004), 20.

3. Schor, 33.

4. "The Serious Side of Eminem," *Rolling Stone*, November 1994, retrieved at www .numberonestars.com/eminem/serious, June 28, 2010.

5. Lifesitenews.com, "Madonna: TV is trash…My kids don't watch TV," October 13, 2005, www.lifesitenews.com/ldn/2005/oct/05101304.html, retrieved February 19, 2010.

6. Madonnaglam.com, "Rosie O'Donnell—It's Like Watching An Olympic Event!" April 24, 2009, http://madonnaglam.i.ph/blogs/madonnaglam/2009/04/24/madonna-rosie -odonnell-it-was-like-watching-an-olympic-event/, retrieved February 19, 2010.

7. Bob Smithouser, *Movie Nights for Teens: 25 More Movies to Spark Spiritual Discussions with Your Teen* (Wheaton, IL: Tyndale House Publishers, 2005), 2.

8. Victor Strasburger, MD, "Clueless: Why Do Pediatricians Underestimate the Media's Influence on Children and Adolescents?" *Pediatrics: Official Journal of the American Academy of Pediatrics,* vol. 117, no. 4, April 2006.

9. *Mind Over Media* video, produced by Focus on the Family, Colorado Springs, CO, 2000.

10. Pluggedinline.com, "Album Reviews: Lady Gaga, The Fame Monster," www.plug gedin.com/music/albums/2010/ladygaga-thefamemonster.aspx, retrieved February 19, 2010.

11. *Redbook,* July 1, 2005.

12. The *Daily Mail,* March 22, 2004.

Chapter Nine—Way #4: Unbrand Her When the World Tries to Buy and Sell Her

1. Taken from styledash.com, retrieved August 15, 2008, and *The Independent,* September 24, 2006.

Chapter Ten—Way #5: Become the Carpool Queen and Sleepover Diva

1. Mitchell J. Prinstein and Kenneth A. Dodge, eds., *Understanding Peer Influences in Children and Adolescents* (New York: The Guildford Press, 2008), 4.

2. Beth Moore, *Feathers from My Nest* (Nashville, TN: Broadman & Holman, 2005), 9.

3. "Should Parents Decide if You Can—or Can't—Be Friends with Someone?" *Discovery Girls,* December/January 2008, 20.

4. Jennifer Kabbany, "Mothers Band Together to Pray for Kids, Schools," *North County Times,* April 24, 2009, retrieved March 4, 2010.

Chapter Eleven—Way # 6: Dream with Her About Her Prince

1. Unfortunately, this book is out of print, though you can often purchase a used copy from sellers on the internet.

2. Julia Fein Azoulay, "The changing scene of the American tween," *Children's Business,* March 1, 2003, retrieved from www.highbeam.com/doc/1G1-99120193.html on 7/24/07.

3. Dr. James Dobson, *Solid Answers* (Wheaton, IL: Tyndale House Publishers, 1997), 197.

4. Jimmy Hester, ed., *Christian Sex Education* (Nashville, Lifeway, 1995), 42.

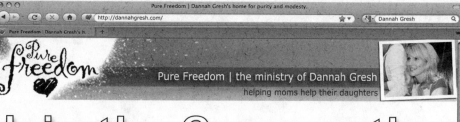

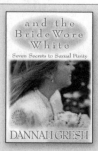
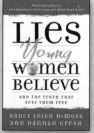

Mirror, mirror on the wall, who has the truest heart of all?

820413117290

Sweetpea Beauty knows that what's on the inside is what matters most, but insecure Queen Blueberry can't see past her own reflection! Will Sweetpea and her friends be able to warn the Queen in time to save her from the clutches of the tricky mirror – or will the crumbling kingdom and the Queen's own heart be lost forever?

bigidea.com

More Great Parenting Resources

THE MOM I WANT TO BE

Rising Above Your Past to Give Your Kids a Great Future

T. SUZANNE ELLER

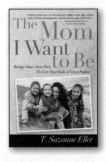

Your experience as a mother and a woman is influenced by the mothering you received as a child. If neglect or inconsistency was a part of your upbringing, you need a healthy vision of the wonderful thing motherhood can be. From her own difficult experience, Suzie Eller shows you ...

- how shattered legacies can be put back together
- ways to forgive, let go, and leave your parenting baggage in the past
- how to give your kids the gift of good memories and a great future

52 THINGS KIDS NEED FROM A DAD

What Fathers Can Do to Make a Lifelong Difference

JAY PAYLEITNER

Good news—you are already the perfect dad for your kids! Still, you know you can grow. Jay Payleitner offers a bounty of inspiring and unexpected insights that show you how God—our heavenly Father—designed fatherhood to be a blast!

- *straightforward rules* like "carry photos of your kids" and "kiss your wife in the kitchen"
- *candid advice* like "get right with your own dad" and "surrender control of the TV remote"
- *weird topics that at first seem absurd:* "buy Peeps" and "rent a dolphin"

Helping Your Kids Deal with Anger, Fear, and Sadness

H. Norman Wright

No parent likes to see their child struggle, especially with dark emotions like anger, fear, and depression. Experienced family counselor and author Norm Wright helps you understand these intense moods and develop sound principles to deal with them effectively.

Parenting Today's Teens
A Practical Devotional

Mark Gregston

Your teenager is facing unprecedented and confusing pressures, temptations, and challenges in today's culture. Mark Gregston has helped teens and their parents through every struggle imaginable, and in these one-page devotions he shares his biblical, practical insights. Here you'll find the wisdom and assurance you need to guide your teen through these years and reach the other side with relationships intact.

When Good Kids Make Bad Choices

Elyse Fitzpatrick and Jim Newheiser with Dr. Laura Hendrickson

How do you as a parent relate to a child who refuses to cooperate, responds in persistent anger or hatred, or rejects the Christian faith? Three qualified biblical counselors share how hurting parents can deal with the emotional trauma caused by a child who goes astray. A compassionate, practical guide that includes helpful advice regarding medicines commonly prescribed to problem children.

10-MINUTE TIME OUTS FOR YOU AND YOUR KIDS

Scripture, Stories, and Prayers You Can Share Together

GRACE FOX

These brief devotions pack excitement and encouragement in a "treasure hunt" through the Bible. In ten minutes a day, you'll

- *read the clue*—share a key verse for the day
- *discover the treasure*—hear a brief story and the truth it portrays
- *share the wealth*—offer a Scripture-based prayer and discuss a question or do the suggested activity
- *hide a jewel*—memorize a verse that reinforces the day's theme

Your family can become rich—filled with the truth about who God is and how He wants His children to live.

To learn more about Harvest House books and
to read sample chapters, log on to our website:

www.harvesthousepublishers.com

HARVEST HOUSE PUBLISHERS
EUGENE, OREGON